Junior Dictionary

First published in 2004 by
Miles Kelly Publishing Ltd
Bardfield Centre, Great Bardfield,
Essex, CM7 4SL

2 4 6 8 10 9 7 5 3 1

Editorial Director: Anne Marshall
Senior Editor: Belinda Gallagher
Editorial Assistant: Lisa Clayden
Designer: Louisa Leitao
Production: Estela Boulton

ISBN 1-84236-418-9

Printed in China

British Library Cataloguing-in-Publication Data
A catalogue record for this book is available from the British Library

www.mileskelly.net
info@mileskelly.net

Junior Dictionary

Cindy Leaney

Miles Kelly PUBLISHING

Junior Dictionary

Your dictionary shows you how to spell words and explains what they mean. It also tells you how to use them. Many words will be familiar – the kind you use every day. Some will be new ones you are just beginning to learn. As you use your dictionary you will find fun things to do and look at. Each letter of the alphabet has its own cartoon, and throughout the book there are puzzles, word games and amazing fact panels.

Definitions
These come after the entry. They explain what the word means.

Example sentences
These sentences follow the definition. They give you an example of the word within a sentence.

Alphabetical order
The words in this book are in alphabetical order. The coloured band along the bottom of every page will tell you which letter of the alphabet you are looking at.

Entries
These are the words in **bold** that you look up. There are more than 1300 entries in your dictionary.

valley ▶ village

Vv

valley
the low land between two hills *There is a river in the valley.*

van
a small truck *The delivery van is here.*

vanish (vanishing, vanished)
to disappear *The deer suddenly vanished.*

vase
a container to hold water in *The vase is hand-painted.*

vegetable
a plant grown for food *Vegetables are healthy foods.*

vehicle
a machine which carries people or things *Trucks and trains are vehicles.*

vest
an undershirt *Put a vest on, it's cold today.*

vet (veterinary surgeon)
an animal doctor *The vet is treating our dog.*

▶ vet

video (video cassette recorder)
a machine for recording or playing TV programmes *Switch the video on.*

village
a group of houses and buildings in the country *It's a beautiful old village.*

▼ vase

A B C D E F G H I J K L N

Illustrations and photographs
These help you to understand the meaning of a word. Each illustration or photograph has its own label to tell you exactly what it is.

Different forms of a word

Some entries are followed by the same word in plural form. This is when there is more than one of something. Usually this just means adding an 's'. If a plural is more complicated, for example, the plural of 'volcano' is 'volcano**es**', it is shown after the entry within brackets.

inegar
 liquid that is used to preserve 'ood, or add flavour *Put vinegar on your chips.*

violin
a musical instrument that is played with a bow *My brother is learning to play the violin.*

▶ violin

virus (viruses)
1 a very tiny living thing that causes disease and illness *Flu is caused by a virus.*
2 a computer program that can damage files *The virus has damaged my files.*

visit (visiting, visited)
to go to see a person or a place *You can visit us this evening.*

voice
the sounds a person makes when speaking or singing *I didn't recognise your voice.*

volcano (volcanoes)
a mountain with an opening that sprays out steam or lava *The volcano is very active.*

vote (voting, voted)
to show which idea or person you choose by raising your hand or writing on paper *Let's take a vote on this idea.*

How many things can you see beginning with 'v'?

N O P Q R S T U V W X Y Z

If an entry is a verb (doing word) then other forms of the word will appear in brackets. For example, the verb **vote** is followed by different endings.

· Did you know? ·

Look for the orange panels to find out interesting facts about the words in your book.

· Puzzle time ·

These are fun things to do and give you a chance to play with words. This helps you to learn and remember them. Puzzle time activities are in green panels.

Cartoons

Look out for the fun cartoons that appear in each letter. How many different things can you see starting with the same letter?

Aa

above

1 in a higher place *Annie lives in the flat above us.*
2 more than *This ride is for children aged six and above.*

accident

something that happens by chance *I dropped it by accident.*

actor (actress, actresses)

a person who plays a part in a film or play *Charlie Chaplin was an actor.*

▶ actor

add (adding, added)

1 to put something together with something else *Add the eggs and sugar.*
2 to put numbers together to find the total *Add six to four to make ten.*

▲ adult

adult

a grown-up, not a child *Only adults are allowed in the pool after six p.m.*

adventure

an exciting experience *Catching the plane by myself was a real adventure.*

advertisement

words or pictures in a newspaper or magazine, or on television or radio, about things for sale *There is an address on the advertisement.*

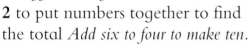

A B C D E F G H I J K L M

aerial
a piece of metal or wire for receiving or sending radio or television signals *There is an aerial on our roof.*

aeroplane
a large machine, with wings and an engine, that flies *Sometimes aeroplanes fly over our house.*

afraid
a feeling of fear, or that something bad is going to happen *Are you afraid of snakes?*

afternoon
part of the day between midday and the evening *We'll go out this afternoon.*

again
to do something once more *Can you say that again?*

age
the number of years someone has lived *At what age can I learn to drive?*

▼ aeroplane

aircraft
machines that fly *Helicopters, planes and microlights are kinds of aircraft.*

airport
a place where aeroplanes land and take off *The airport is very busy.*

alarm
a machine that flashes or makes a noise as a warning *The burglar alarm is flashing!*

N O P Q R S T U V W X Y Z

alien

something strange that comes from another planet *E.T. is a friendly alien.*

alligator

an animal with a long tail and big teeth that lives around rivers and lakes *Alligators lay eggs.*

alphabet

letters in a special order that form a language *The English alphabet starts with A and ends with Z.*

a b c d e f g h i j k l m n o
p q r s t u v w x y z

ambulance

a vehicle for taking people who are ill or hurt to and from the hospital *Cars pull to one side when an ambulance is coming.*

angry

a feeling that something is wrong or unfair *I am angry with you.*

animal

a living thing that can move *Humans, fish, birds and snakes are all animals.*

ankle

part of the body between the leg and the foot that bends *I have twisted my ankle.*

answer

1 something you say or write after a question *My answer is no.*
2 the correct reply to a question or correct result to a problem. *That's the right answer!*

◀ ambulance

A B C D E F G H I J K L M

answer (answering, answered)
1 to say or write something when asked a question *You must answer the questions.*
2 to pick up the telephone or go to the door *Answer the door!*

ant
an insect that lives in groups *There is a line of ants marching into the sugar bowl!*

appear (appearing, appeared)
1 to look or to seem *She appears to be much better.*
2 to come into sight *Our sister suddenly appeared.*

apple
a fruit that grows on trees *Apples are red, yellow or green.*

▶ apple

apricot
a small, fuzzy-skinned yellow fruit *I like dried apricots on cereal.*

apron
a piece of cloth that you put on top of your clothes to keep them clean. *Put an apron on before you open the paint tin.*

▲ How many things can you see beginning with 'a'?

aquarium
a plastic or glass box filled with water for keeping fish in *The fish swim in the aquarium.*

N O P Q R S T U V W X Y Z

argue (arguing, argued)
to strongly disagree *Don't argue, it's not important.*

arm
the part of your body that is positioned between your shoulder and hand *My right arm is stronger than my left arm.*

armchair
a chair that has places for you to rest your arms *I like to read when I'm sitting in an armchair.*

army
the people that fight for a country on land *The ancient Roman army was very powerful.*

arrest (arresting, arrested)
to take someone away and guard them *The police arrested two people.*

art
the making of paintings, drawings and sculpture *There is an art show at school.*

artist
a person who makes art *Picasso was a famous artist.*

▶ artist

ask (asking, asked)
to say to someone you want them to tell you something, or do something for you *You should ask for help.*

asleep
sleeping *Shhh, please be quiet, the baby is fast asleep.*

astronaut
a person who travels into space in a spacecraft *Astronauts sometimes spend months on a space station.*

athlete
a person who plays a sport *Athletes train every day.*

▶ athlete

attack (attacking, attacked)
to be violent *Pirates attacked the ship.*

aunt
the sister of your mother or father, the wife of your uncle *My aunt looks like my mother.*

autograph
the name of a famous person, written by them *Can I have your autograph?*

automatic
a machine that works by itself *The washing machine is automatic.*

autumn
the time of year between the summer and the winter *The leaves turn red in autumn.*

awake
not sleeping, not asleep *I tried to stay awake all night.*

awful
very bad *This medicine tastes awful.*

axe
a tool with a handle and a sharp piece of metal at the end that is used for chopping wood and cutting down trees *Dad uses an axe to chop wood.*

▶ axe

N O P Q R S T U V W X Y Z

baboon

a large monkey
Baboons are very noisy.

▼ baby

baby (babies)

a young child that
has not yet learned
to talk or walk
*The baby's name is
Alex.*

back

1 part of your body behind you,
between your shoulders and hips
I can swim on my back.
2 the part of something that is
furthest from the front or from the
way it is facing *The wires are at the
back of the computer.*

backwards

the direction opposite to the way
something is facing *Take four steps
backwards.*

bacon

meat from a pig *We have bacon and
eggs for breakfast.*

bad (worse, worst)

not good or pleasant *It's bad news.*

badge

a piece of paper, plastic, metal or
cloth that you put on your clothes
to say who you are or what you
have done *I have four swimming
badges.*

▶ badger

badger

an animal with
black and white
fur that lives
underground
*There is a family of
badgers living in the wood.*

badly

not done well *I play the piano badly.*

A B C D E F G H I J K L M

badminton

a game such as tennis that is played with rackets and a small object with feathers *We play badminton every day.*

bag

a container made of plastic, paper, cloth or leather *Put the vegetables into one bag.*

baggy

loose, not tight *I like baggy sweaters.*

bake (baking, baked)

to cook food in an oven *Bake the cake for 40 minutes.*

balcony

an area outside a window where you can sit or stand *You can see the beach from the balcony.*

bald

without hair *My dad is going bald.*

ball

an object that you throw, hit or kick in games *Throw the ball in the air.*

ballet

a type of dancing that tells a story with no words *A very famous ballet is* Swan Lake.

balloon

a rubber bag filled with air that is used as a decoration *We had balloons at the party.*

banana

a long, curved yellow fruit *I like bananas for breakfast.*

▶ bananas

bang

a sudden loud noise *The door shut with a bang.*

N O P Q R S T U V W X Y Z

bank

1 a place to keep money *There is a bank in the town.*
2 the land alongside a river *People sit on the bank and fish.*

▲ How many things can you see beginning with 'b'?

barn

a farm building for keeping animals or crops *The cows are in the barn.*

basket

a container made of thin strips, to hold or carry things *Put the bread in the basket.*

basketball

a game played by two teams who try to get points by throwing a ball through a round net *Basketball is a fast game.*

bat

1 a small animal that usually flies at night *Bats have good hearing.*
2 the wooden stick used to hit a ball in games such as baseball and cricket *Baseball bats are rounded, cricket bats are flat.*

bath

a long container that you fill with water and sit in to wash your body *There's nothing more relaxing than a warm bath at the end of the day.*

beach (beaches)

the area of land that is right next to the sea *Would you like to come for a picnic on the beach?*

A B C D E F G H I J K L M

bean

the seed of a climbing plant that is eaten as food *I like baked beans on toast.*

▶ bear

bear

a large, strong wild animal that is covered in fur *Bears have long, sharp claws.*

beard

hair that grows on a man's chin and cheeks *My Dad has a beard.*

beautiful

very pleasant *Roses are beautiful.*

bed

a piece of furniture for sleeping on *There are two beds in my room.*

bee

a yellow and black striped insect *Bees live in a nest called a hive.*

Puzzle time

Untangle the bees to see which one gets home

begin (beginning, began)

to start *Begin at the top of the page.*

behind

at the back of someone or something *She's hiding behind the garden fence.*

N O P Q R S T U V W X Y Z

bell

1 a hollow, metal object that makes a sound when hit *Press the bell for service.*
2 a machine that makes a ringing sound *The bell rings at 3:15 p.m.*

below

in a lower place than something else *The gym is on the floor below.*

belt

a piece of clothing that you wear around your waist *Belts can be made of leather, cloth or plastic.*

bench (benches)

a seat for two or more people to sit on *Wait on the bench.*

better (best)

something of a higher standard or quality *The new game is better than the last one.*

between

in a place or time that separates two things or people *You can sit between us.*

handlebars   ▼ bike

saddle

wheel

pedal

chain

bicycle (bike)

a machine with two wheels that you sit on and move by pushing on pedals to make the wheels go round *I'd like a new bicycle for my birthday.*

big (bigger, biggest)

1 large, not small *The shirt is too big.*
2 important *Tomorrow is a big day.*

A B C E D F G H I J K L M

bird

an animal that has wings, feathers and lays eggs *Most birds can fly.*

▶ bird

birthday

the day of the year on which a person is born *When is your birthday?*

biscuit

a dry, thin cake that is usually sweet *Would you like a biscuit?*

bite (biting, bit, bitten)

to cut into something with your teeth *Have a bite of the apple.*

▶ bite

bitter

having a strong, sharp taste such as coffee *Add sugar, it tastes bitter.*

blanket

a piece of material on a bed that you use to keep warm *There's a blanket on the bed.*

blind

not able to see *Talking books are made for blind people.*

blister

a raised piece of skin, filled with liquid, caused by burning or rubbing *I have a blister on my foot.*

blizzard

a very heavy snow storm *People shouldn't drive in a blizzard.*

blood

liquid that the heart pumps through your body *The colour of blood is dark red.*

N O P Q R S T U V W X Y Z

bloom (blooming, bloomed)
to open out into a flower *There are flowers blooming all over the garden.*

blow (blowing, blew)
to push air out of your mouth *It's fun to blow bubbles!*

boat
a small ship *You get to the island by boat.*

body (bodies)
1 the whole of a person *Skin covers your body.*
2 a dead person *They covered the body with a blanket.*

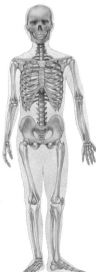

▶ bones

bone
a hard, white part under the skin of a person or animal *Your skeleton has more than 200 bones.*

book
1 sheets of paper with writing on, joined together for reading *This is a book about spiders.*
2 sheets of paper joined together for writing on *Write your name on the cover of your exercise book.*

boot
1 a shoe that covers your foot and ankle *Wear your boots in the rain.*
2 part of a car for carrying things *The bags are in the boot.*

▲ boots

bored
not interested *I'm bored, let's play a game.*

born
to start life *When were you born?*

A B C D E F G H I J K L M

borrow (borrowing, borrowed)
to have something that belongs to
another person and return
it to them *You can borrow
the books for two weeks.*

bottle
a tall container for
storing liquid *I have a
water bottle on my bike.*

▶ bottles

· Did you know? ·
People discovered how to
make glass containers more
than 2000 years ago!

bottom
the lowest part of something *The
number is at the bottom of the page.*

bounce (bouncing, bounced)
1 to move back quickly after hitting
or falling on something *Bounce on the
trampoline.*
2 to throw an object against
something so it moves back quickly
Bounce the ball against the wall.

bow
1 a knot with loops *Tie a bow on top
of the present.*
2 a long, thin stick with string for
shooting arrows or playing an
instrument *You play the violin with a
bow.*

bow (bowing, bowed)
to bend your body or your head to
show respect *The servants all bowed
to the king.*

bowl
a deep, curved dish *You eat cereal out
of a bowl.*

N O P Q R S T U V W X Y Z

box (boxes)
a container with four sides *Keep the crayons in a box.*

boxing
the sport of fighting with closed hands *There is a boxing match on TV.*

boy
a male child or a young man *There are two boys in their family.*

bracelet
a piece of jewellery worn around the wrist *My bracelet has my name on it.*

brain
the part of your body inside your head that you use for thinking, feeling and moving *When you touch something hot, nerves send a message to your brain and you pull your hand away.*

branch
the part of a tree that grows out from the trunk *Leaves, flowers and fruit grow on branches.*

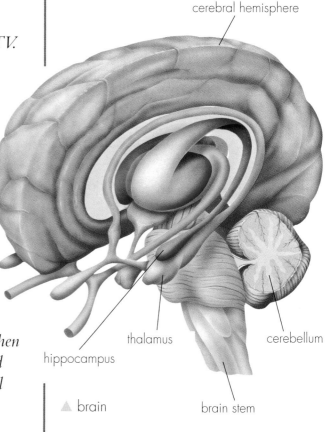

cerebral hemisphere

thalamus

cerebellum

hippocampus

brain stem

▲ brain

A B C D E F G H I J K L M
▲

bread
a type of food made with flour, water and yeast *Have some bread.*

break (breaking, broke, broken)
to make something separate into two or more pieces *I've broken a glass.*

breakfast
the first meal of the day *We had cereal for breakfast.*

breeze
a light wind *There's a breeze blowing.*

brick
a block of baked clay used for building *The wall is made from bricks.*

bridge
a structure built to join two things *There is a bridge over the river.*

▶ bridge

bright
1 full of light *It's a bright, sunny day.*
2 strong and easy to see *Wear bright colours when you go into the forest.*
3 clever, intelligent *That's a bright idea.*

brilliant
1 very bright and strong *The North Star is brilliant.*
2 very good at doing something *She's a brilliant scientist.*
3 very good or enjoyable *It's a brilliant game!*

N O P Q R S T U V W X Y Z

bring (bringing, brought)
to take something with you *Why don't you come over tonight and bring a friend with you?*

broccoli
a green vegetable *Let's have broccoli with our dinner.*

broom
a brush with a handle *Sweep the floor with a broom.*

brother
a boy or a man who has the same parents as another person *Nadia has two brothers.*

brush (brushes)
a tool that has stiff hairs fastened to a handle that is used for sweeping, painting, cleaning or smoothing *It's always best to wash your paintbrushes in cold water.*

bucket
a round, open container with a handle *Put the water in a bucket.*

build (building, built)
to make something, such as a house, by putting pieces together *There are plans to build a new school next year.*

•Puzzle time•

Which of these brushes is the odd one out?

answer:
broom

A B C D E F G H I J K L M

building

a man-made place, usually with a roof and walls *The Taj Mahal is a building in India.*

▶ building

bull

a male cow, elephant or whale *There's a bull running loose in that field.*

burglar

a person who goes into buildings to steal things *A burglar stole the money.*

burn (burning, burned, burnt)

1 to be on fire *The candles are burning.* **2** to destroy something with fire *The shed burnt down.*

bus (buses)

a vehicle that carries passengers *The bus stops at our road.*

bush (bushes)

a small tree *Berries grow on bushes.*

butter

yellow food that is made from milk *Spread butter on the bread.*

butterfly (butterflies)

an insect with large wings *Butterflies drink from flowers.*

◀ butterfly

button

a round object that fastens clothes *The dress has one button.*

buy (buying, bought)

to get something by paying money for it *Shall we buy some sweets?*

N O P Q R S T U V W X Y Z

Cc

▶ cabbage

cabbage
a large vegetable with thick, round leaves *Rabbits love eating cabbages.*

cabin
1 a small house made of wood, usually in the country *The cabin is halfway up the mountain.*
2 the place where the passengers sit inside an aeroplane *The pilot walked back through the cabin.*
3 a small room to sleep in on a ship *The cabin has two beds.*

cactus (cacti, cactuses)
a plant that grows in hot, dry places that has needles instead of leaves *The needles on a cactus are sharp.*

▶ cactus

café
a place that serves drinks and simple meals *Why don't we stop and have lunch at a café?*

cage
a room or box made of bars in which to keep animals or birds *Pet hamsters and mice live in cages.*

cake
a sweet food made of flour, sugar and eggs that is baked in an oven *Mum baked me a chocolate cake for my birthday.*

calendar
a special chart that shows the days, weeks and months of the year *We wrote everyone's birthday on the calendar.*

A B C D E F G H I J K L M

calf (calves)

1 a baby cow, elephant or whale *The calf is two days old.*
2 the back part of your leg between your ankle and knee *I've pulled a muscle in my calf.*

▼ calf

call (calling, called)

1 to shout or say something in a loud voice *Dad calls us in for dinner at six o'clock.*
2 to telephone *Call me when you get home.*
3 to visit *The doctor calls when someone is very ill.*
4 to give someone or something a name *They called the baby Luke.*

camel

a large animal with one or two humps that can carry heavy loads *A camel can go without water for a long time.*

▶ camel

camera

a piece of equipment used for taking photographs or filming *You get a digital camera free with this computer.*

camp

a place where people stay in tents *The camp is over the hill.*

camp (camping, camped)

to stay in a tent *Every summer the scouts camp in this field.*

can

a metal container *We collect drink cans for charity.*

N O P Q R S T U V W X Y Z

can (could)
1 to be able to do something *Aziz can use the Internet.*
2 to be allowed to do something *We can come to your party.*

▶ candle

candle
a stick of wax with a string through it that you burn for light *There are nine candles on her birthday cake.*

captain
1 someone who leads a team *Who is captain of the football team this year?*
2 a person who is in charge of a ship or a plane *The captain says the flight will take two hours.*

▶ car

car
a machine on wheels that has an engine and that people can ride in *There is a car in the driveway.*

caravan
a small house on wheels that can be pulled behind a car *David and Katya have taken the caravan on holiday.*

card
1 thick, stiff paper *Use a piece of card to make a sign from.*
2 a piece of card with words and a picture that you give or send someone *My brother gave me a birthday card to open.*
3 a piece of stiff paper or plastic that you use to buy things or to identify yourself *I have a library card.*
4 a piece of stiff paper with pictures and numbers that you use to play games *Give each player seven cards.*

A B C D E F G H I J K L M

cardigan

a piece of clothing such as a sweater with buttons down the front *Wear a cardigan if it's cold.*

careful (carefully)

paying attention to what you are doing so that you don't make a mistake or have an accident *Be careful! That knife is sharp.*

carpet

a thick cover for the floor *The carpet in my bedroom is green and blue.*

carrot

a long, orange vegetable that grows under the ground *Carrots are a very healthy food to eat.*

carry (carrying, carried)

to move something from one place to another *Can you help me carry all the shopping indoors?*

cassette

a plastic box with a tape inside it for recording or playing back sound or video *Put the cassette into the stereo.*

castle

a large, strong building with thick walls *Castles were built to keep the people inside safe from their enemies.*

· **Did you know?** ·

Berkeley Castle is said to be haunted by the ghost of King Edward II.

▶ cat

cat

a small, furry animal with a long tail and sharp claws *My cat likes to climb trees.*

catch (catching, caught)
1 to get hold of something *Catch the ball!*
2 to get an illness *People often catch cold in winter.*
3 to get on a bus, train, plane or ferry and go somewhere *We usually catch the bus to the airport.*

▲ How many things can you see beginning with 'c'?

caterpillar
an animal, like a worm with legs, that turns into a butterfly or a moth *Caterpillars eat leaves.*

cave
a hole in a mountainside or under the ground *Caves are usually dark.*

CD (CDs, compact disc)
a circular piece of plastic for storing sound *Have you bought their latest CD? It's really good!*

CD-ROM (CD-ROMs, compact disc read-only memory)
a circular piece of plastic for storing information to be used by a computer *CD-ROMs hold lots of information.*

celery
a vegetable that is often used in salads *Celery is crunchy.*

cereal
a breakfast food that is made from plants such as wheat, oats and rice *Pour some milk on the cereal.*

chair
a piece of furniture for sitting on *Pull your chair close to the desk.*

A B C D E F G H I J K L M

chalk

a soft, white rock *We used different coloured chalk to draw the picture.*

chameleon

a lizard that changes colour so its skin matches the things around it *Chameleons eat flies.*

change (changing, changed)

1 to become different or to make something different *You haven't changed at all!*
2 to put on different clothes *I'll be downstairs as soon as I've changed into something warmer.*

cheap (cheaper, cheapest)

not expensive *This watch is cheap but it is well-made.*

cheese

a food that is made from milk *Can I have some cheese on toast for supper?*

cherry (cherries)

a small, round reddish fruit that has a stone in the centre *We'll have cherry pie for dessert.*

▲ cherries

chest

1 the part of your body between your neck and your stomach *Place the belt across your chest.*
2 a strong box with a top that locks *The chest was filled with gold!*

chicken

a farm bird that is kept for eggs and meat *Chickens can't fly very far.*

child (children)

1 a young person *He's just a child.*
2 someone's son or daughter *They love all their children.*

N O P Q R S T U V W X Y Z

chimney

an opening over a fire that takes smoke out through the roof of a building *The chimney is filled with soot.*

chin

part of your face under your mouth *His beard hides his chin.*

chips

pieces of potato fried in oil *Do you like fish and chips?*

chocolate

a sweet food made from cocoa beans *Would you like some chocolate?*

Christmas

a Christian holiday *Where are you spending Christmas?*

church (churches)

the place where Christians meet to worship *The church is full of flowers.*

cinema

a place you go to see films *Shall we go to the cinema?*

circus (circuses)

a show with people and animals, held in a big tent *The circus is in town!*

▶ circus

A B C D E F G H I J K L M

city (cities)
a large town *It is a big, busy city.*

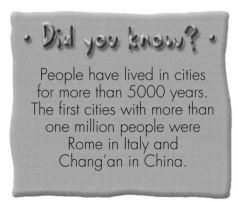

· Did you know? ·
People have lived in cities for more than 5000 years. The first cities with more than one million people were Rome in Italy and Chang'an in China.

clap (clapping, clapped)
to make a loud sound by hitting the palms of your hands together *The actors bowed and we clapped louder.*

class (classes)
1 a group of people who learn together *We're in the same class.*
2 a group of things or animals that are the same *People belong to the class of animals called mammals.*

claw
a sharp, hard part of an animal's foot *Cats have sharp claws.*

clean
not dirty *The car is clean and shiny.*

clean (cleaning, cleaned)
to make something tidy, to take dirt away *Clean your room!*

clear
1 easy to understand, hear or read *The instructions are clear.*
2 easy to see through *You can see the fish swimming in the clear water.*

clever
able to learn or understand things quickly *Well done – you're very clever.*

cliff
the side of a rock or mountain *The road runs along a cliff.*

N O P Q R S T U V W X Y Z

climb (climbing, climbed)
to move upwards *She climbed to the top.*

clock
a machine that tells the time *The clock said 5:55 a.m.*

close
near *The hotel is close to the beach.*

▶ clock

close (closing, closed)
to shut *Close the window, I'm cold.*

cloth
1 a soft material *The chair is covered in cloth.*
2 a piece of cloth for a special purpose *Clean the window with a cloth.*

clothes
things that people wear *Shirts, jeans and skirts are all clothes.*

cloud
a white or grey object in the sky that is made of tiny drops of water *It's a beautiful day, just a few clouds.*

clown
someone who makes people laugh *Harry is our class clown.*

▶ clown

coast
the land next to the sea *The village is on the coast.*

coat
a piece of clothing you wear over your clothes to stay warm or keep the rain off *This is a warm coat.*

A B C D E F G H I J K L M

coconut
the nut of the palm tree *Coconuts give delicious juice.*

cocoon
the bag around an insect that protects it while it is growing into an adult *The cocoon broke open and a butterfly flew out.*

coffee
the brown beans of a plant, or a hot drink that can be made from them *I'm making a hot drink, would you prefer tea or coffee?*

coin
a piece of money that is made of metal *They keep coins from their holidays.*

cold
not warm or hot *Brrr – this water is very cold.*

collect (collecting, collected)
to put things together in one place *Some people collect coins.*

▲ colour

colour
blue, green, red or yellow *What colour is your jacket?*

colour (colouring, coloured)
to make something a colour with paint, crayons or ink *We coloured the picture in.*

comb
an object for making your hair tidy *Don't let anyone use your comb.*

N O P Q R S T U V W X Y Z

comic

a magazine with pictures that tell a story *Comics are often funny.*

compass

an object that shows you what direction you are travelling in *Read the compass to find the treasure!*

▲ compass

competition

a test to see who is best at something *There was a singing competition on the radio.*

complain (complaining, complained)

to say that something is wrong and you are not happy about it *He complained to the waiter.*

computer

a machine for storing information and doing jobs such as sums and writing letters *You can play games on computers.*

confused

a feeling of not being sure *I was confused by the question.*

container

something that holds something else in it *Jars, tins and boxes are containers.*

cook

to make food hot so it can be eaten *Ahmed is cooking dinner for us.*

cool

a little bit cold *There is a cool breeze.*

copy (copying, copied)

to do something the same as something else *Copy the writing.*

A B C D E F G H I J K L M

corn
1 a plant with large, yellow seeds
This corn is delicious.
2 the seeds of plants such
as wheat and oats
*Many farmers grow
different types of corn
every year.*

▶ corn

cough
(coughing, coughed)
to force air from your throat *She's
still coughing, give her a drink of water.*

count (counting, counted)
to find out how many *Count the
children in the playground.*

▶ crab

country (countries)
1 a place with its own government
Which country do you live in?
2 away from cities and towns *We live
in a village in the country.*

cousin
the child of your aunt or uncle
Charlie is my cousin.

cow (cattle, cows)
a large, female farm animal that
gives milk *Cows eat grass.*

cowboy
a man who rides a horse and takes
care of cattle *The cowboy tried to ride
the horse.*

crab
a sea animal that moves
sideways and has big
claws *Crabs are good
to eat.*

N O P Q R S T U V W X Y Z

crack
where something is broken *There's a crack in this mug.*

crack (cracking, cracked)
to break something so that a line appears on it *Just crack the shell.*

crash (crashing, crashed)
1 to have an accident *The car crashed into a tree.*
2 to make a loud noise *Hear the thunder crash!*

crawl (crawling, crawled)
to move around on your hands and knees *The baby is starting to crawl.*

crayon
a coloured wax stick *Can I use your crayons?*

creep (creeping, crept)
to move so that no one sees or hears you *Oh! Don't creep up on me!*

crisps
fried, thin slices of potato *I love eating crisps.*

crocodile
a large animal with a long body, short legs and big teeth that lives in rivers and lakes *Crocodiles live in hot countries.*

◀ crocodile

crooked
not straight *The fence is very crooked.*

crop
plants that are grown for people and animals to eat, or that are used to make things *The weather is very important to farmers who grow crops.*

cross
two lines that go over each other
There is a cross on the map where the treasure is hidden.

cross (crossing, crossed)
to go from one side of something to the other *Cross the road carefully.*

▶ crown

crown
a metal circle that kings and queens wear on their heads *The queen and king are both wearing gold crowns.*

cruel
not kind *He's a cruel king.*

crumb
A small piece of something such as bread or cake *Whose eaten the cake? There are only crumbs left.*

cry (crying, cried)
1 to make tears from your eyes, usually because you feel sad or are hurt *Sometimes you feel better after you have cried.*
2 to shout *"Help! Help!" they cried.*

cucumber
a long, thin green vegetable that is used in salads *I'd like a cucumber and tomato salad.*

cuddle (cuddling, cuddled)
to hold someone in your arms to show you care *Chloe cuddled her best friend to cheer her up.*

▶ cuddle

N O P Q R S T U V W X Y Z

cup

a container with a handle for drinking from *Put a teabag in the cup, then add water.*

cupboard

a piece of furniture for storing things *Please dry the dishes and put them in the cupboard.*

curious

wanting to know or find out about something *Cats are very curious.*

curl

something like hair or ribbon that is curved at the end *She has beautiful curls.*

▶ curls

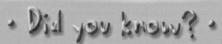

Did you know?

Hair grows from a follicle (pit) in the scalp. Coloured substances called melanin (dark brown) and carotene (yellowish) give hair its colour. Black, curly hair is the result of black melanin growing from a flat follicle.

curtain

cloth that hangs across or over a window *Pull the curtains at night.*

cushion

a bag with soft material inside for sitting or lying on *Put a cushion under your head.*

cut (cutting, cut)

to remove something with a knife or scissors *I'm going to get my hair cut.*

A B C D E F G H I J K L M

daisy (daisies)
a flower with white petals and a yellow centre *You can make a chain of daisies.*

dance (dancing, danced)
to move your body to music *This music is good to dance to.*

dangerous
not safe *Playing with matches is dangerous.*

dark
not light *It's too dark to play outside.*

daughter
a female child *My daughter isn't well.*

day
1 a 24-hour period *We're staying for three days.*
2 from the time the sun rises until it sets *Bats do not fly during the day.*

▲ daisies

dead
not alive *This plant looks dead.*

deaf
not able to hear *Many deaf people can read lips.*

dear
1 a word to start a letter *Dear Aran, How are you?*
2 much cared about *She's a very dear friend.*
3 expensive *The dress is too dear.*

N O P Q R S T U V W X Y Z

deep
a long way from the top to the bottom, or from the front to the back *I'm not afraid to swim in the deep end of the pool.*

deer (deer)
an animal that lives in forests *Deer are gentle animals.*

delicious
tasting very good *This ice cream is delicious.*

delighted
very happy *I'm delighted with my new bike.*

▶ dessert

dentist
a person who looks after people's teeth *I go to the dentist twice a year.*

desert
a place where there is very little or no rain *Most deserts are hot.*

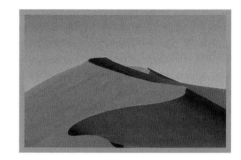

▲ desert

desk
a piece of furniture that you sit at to read, write or use a computer *There's a lamp on my desk.*

dessert
sweet food that you eat at the end of a meal *What's for dessert?*

detective
a person who finds information about a crime or another person *Some police officers are detectives.*

A B C D E F G H I J K L M

diary
a book with the days of the year in it that you use to write down what you plan to do, or what you have done *I write in my diary before I go to bed each night.*

die (dice)
a cube with spots on each side that is used for playing games *It's your turn – throw the dice.*

die (dying, died)
to stop living *Water the plant before it dies.*

different
not the same *These two sweets look the same but they taste different.*

difficult
not easy *I hope the spelling test isn't too difficult.*

dig (digging, dug)
to make a hole in the earth or to move it *Big machines can dig faster than we can.*

▶ digger

digital
1 showing information using numbers that can change *This is a digital watch.*
2 storing information using only zero and one *Most music is digitally recorded these days.*

dining room
the room in which you eat your meals *The dining room is next to the kitchen in our house.*

dinner
the main evening meal *What's for dinner?*

dinosaur
an animal that became extinct 65 million years ago *One type of dinosaur was* Tyrannosaurus Rex.

dirty
not clean, messy *We put dirty clothes in the washing basket.*

disabled
a disabled person cannot use part of their body *This parking space is for disabled drivers only.*

disappear (disappearing, disappeared)
to go out of sight or become impossible to find *The sun disappeared behind a cloud.*

disco
a place or a party where people dance *There's a disco on Saturday.*

Seismosaurus

Ankylosaurus

Stegosaurus

Diplodocus

▲ dinosaurs

Stenonychosaurus

A B C D E F G H I J K L M

discover (discovering, discovered)

to find or understand something for the first time *Alexander Fleming discovered penicillin, a type of medicine.*

disease

a serious illness *Flu is a disease.*

disguise

something that you wear to hide who you really are *He's in disguise.*

dish (dishes)

something like a bowl or plate, used for serving food *Please dry the dishes.*

disk

a piece of plastic for storing computer information *Save the file on a disk.*

dive (diving, dived)

to go into water headfirst *I can dive.*

dizzy

the feeling that things are turning around you or that you are going to fall *That ride makes me dizzy.*

doctor

a person who looks after sick people or helps stop people from being ill *Doctors work very hard.*

▶ doctor

document

1 papers that contain official information *Important documents are filed away.*
2 a piece of work that is saved in a file on a computer *You can attach a document to an email.*

N O P Q R S T U V W X Y Z

dog

an animal that people keep as a pet *Our dog is a sheep dog.*

doll

a toy in the shape of a person *Let's play with our dolls.*

dolphin

a large, warm-blooded animal that lives in the ocean *A dolphin looks like a fish but it is an air-breathing mammal.*

domino (dominoes)

a piece of black wood or plastic with white spots that is used to play games *Playing dominoes is good for your maths!*

donkey

an animal that looks similar to a small horse with a long tail and big ears *Every day we feed carrots to the donkeys near our house.*

door

something that you open and close to go into or out of a room, house or car *Can you open the door for me?*

down

1 towards a lower place *Get down off the ladder.*
2 at a lower rate or speed *Prices are coming down.*

dragon

▼ dragon

an imaginary animal such as a big lizard that breathes fire *The story is about a princess trapped in a dragon's cave.*

dramatic

surprising or exciting *It's dramatic news.*

A B C D E F G H I J K L M

draw (drawing, drew, drawn)
to make a picture *You can draw well.*

drawer
part of a piece of furniture that slides in and out that is used for storing things *Put all the clothes in the drawer.*

dream (dreaming, dreamt or dreamed)
1 to think about or see things in your sleep *I dreamed that I could fly.*
2 to hope for something *We dream of being famous.*

dress (dressing, dressed)
to put clothes on *Get dressed, we're ready to go.*

dress (dresses)
a piece of clothing for girls or women that has a top and skirt *That's a beautiful dress.*

drink
liquid food *Would you like a drink?*

drink (drinking, drank, drunk)
to take liquid into your mouth and swallow it *Drink lots of water.*

◀ drink

drive (driving, drove, driven)
to control a vehicle, such as a car *My oldest brother can drive.*

drop (dropping, dropped)
to fall or to let something fall *Don't drop that vase.*

N O P Q R S T U V W X Y Z

▶ drum

drum
a musical instrument that you hit with a stick or your hand *He plays the drums.*

• Did you know? •

Giant drums are used in the temple ceremonies of Japan's oldest religion, Shinto. The largest drum measures 1.8 metres across and weighs 4 tonnes.

dry
not wet *The washing is nearly dry.*

duck
a bird with webbed feet that lives near water *We feed bread to the ducks.*

▲ How many things can you see beginning with 'd'?

dustbin
a big container for storing rubbish *The dustbins are emptied on Tuesdays.*

DVD (digital versatile disk)
a circular piece of plastic used for storing and playing music and films *Is the film on DVD?*

A B C **D** **E** F G H I J K L M

Ee

eagle
a bird that hunts for its food *An eagle has sharp claws called talons.*

ear
the part of your body that you use to hear *My ears feel cold.*

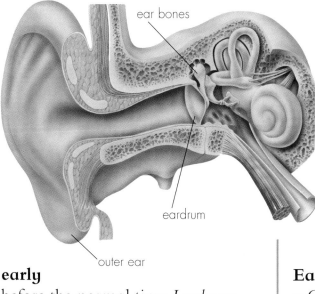

ear bones

eardrum

outer ear

early
before the normal time *I wake up early in the summer.*

earn (earning, earned)
to get money for work *I earn extra pocket money for washing the car.*

earring
a piece of jewellery that is worn on the ear *Can I wear my new earrings?*

◀ ear

Earth (earth)
1 the planet we live on *Earth travels around the Sun.*
2 soil *Sprinkle earth over the seeds.*

earthquake
a strong shaking of the earth *Earthquakes can cause serious damage.*

Easter
a Christian holiday *We're spending Easter at home.*

N O P Q R S T U V W X Y Z

easy
not difficult *This book is easy to read.*

eat (eating, ate, eaten)
to take food into your mouth and swallow it *What shall we have to eat?*

echo (echoes)
a sound that bounces off something and can be heard again *There is a strong echo when you shout into the cave.*

▶ eggs

egg
1 an oval object with a shell that some animals lay, from which their babies hatch *The robin has laid an egg.*
2 an egg used as food *Shall we make fried eggs for breakfast?*

elbow
where your arm bends *Ouch, I bumped my elbow.*

electricity
power that is used to make lights and machines work *Lightning is a giant spark of electricity.*

elephant
a large, wild animal with a long nose called a trunk *A baby elephant is called a calf.*

email
messages sent by computer *I received emails from all my friends.*

empty
with nothing inside *The box is empty.*

end
to finish or stop *The film ends at 6:30 p.m.*

enemy (enemies)
someone who does not like you, or wants to hurt you *We are enemies, not friends.*

energy
strength or power *We're trying to save energy.*

engine
1 a machine that makes something work *Most engines are in the front of cars.*
2 Part of a train that pulls the other carriages *The steam engine is very noisy.*

enjoy (enjoying, enjoyed)
to like to do something *I enjoy playing tennis.*

enormous
very, very big *Whales are enormous animals.*

enough
as much as you need *There is enough for everyone.*

enter (entering, entered)
1 to go into a place *The king entered the hall.*
2 to put information into a computer *The names and addresses are entered in a file.*

engine

N O P Q R S T U V W X Y Z

entrance

the way into a place *The entrance to the cave was very dark.*

envelope

a paper cover for letters and cards *Put a stamp on the envelope.*

▶ envelopes

environment

everything around us, such as land, air or water *They live in a hot environment.*

equal

the same as something else in number, size or amount *One kilogram is equal to 1000 grams.*

equipment

things that are used to do something such as work or sport *Our school has lots of new computer equipment.*

escalator

a staircase that moves *We went up the escalator.*

escape (escaping, escaped)

to leave a place that is dangerous or unpleasant *They escaped from the prison.*

evening

the time of day between afternoon and night time *It starts to get dark in the evening.*

▲ evening

excellent

very good *This is an excellent song.*

A B C D E F G H I J K L M

excited
happy and interested in something
I am excited about tomorrow.

excuse
a reason you give for something
that you have said or done *Her
excuse for being late is that she overslept.*

exercise
movements that you make to stay fit
and healthy *Exercise keeps you fit.*

exhibition
a show where people can look at
things like paintings *There is an
exhibition of our artwork at school.*

exit
the way to leave a place *There is a
light over the exit.*

expensive
costing a lot *Jewellery can be expensive.*

explain (explaining, explained)
to say what something means or
why it has happened *Our teacher
explained how the equipment worked.*

explanation
what something means or why it
happened *There is a good explanation
for the accident.*

▲ How many things can you see
beginning with 'e'?

explode (exploding, exploded)
to suddenly burst or blow up into
small pieces *The fireworks exploded in
the night sky.*

N O P Q R S T U V W X Y Z

explore (exploring, explored)
to look around a new place *We explored the cave.*

explosion
the noise, smoke, and sometimes flames, that are made when something blows up into pieces *The explosion filled the air with smoke.*

extinct
no longer existing *The dodo is an extinct bird.*

◀ extinct

extra
more than is necessary *People are nice to you on your birthday.*

eye
the part of the body that animals use to see *What colour are your eyes?*

• Did you know? •
Your eyes measure only 2.5 centimetres across, but they can see things as far away as a star in space and objects as tiny as a grain of sand.

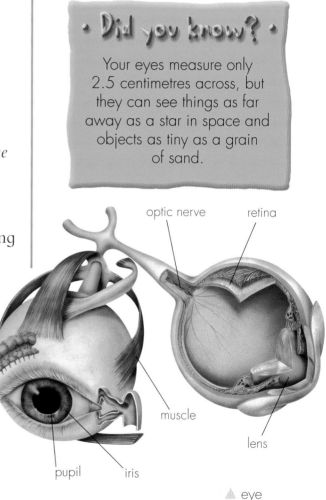

optic nerve   retina

muscle

lens

pupil   iris

▲ eye

A B C D E F G H I J K L M

face

the front part of your head *She has such a pretty face.*

▶ face

factory

a place where things are made in large numbers by machines and people *Dad works at the car factory.*

faint

1 not strong or easy to hear, see or smell *There is a faint smell of smoke.*
2 feeling weak and light-headed *I am so hungry I feel faint.*

fair

1 good and reasonable *Their decision is fair.*
2 light-coloured *He has fair hair*
3 fine, pleasant *If the weather is fair, we'll go to the beach.*

fairy (fairies)

a magical person with wings *Tinkerbell is the fairy in* Peter Pan.

▶ fairy

fairy tale

a story for children about magical things *Some fairy tales are very old.*

fake

not real *Her coat is fake fur.*

fall (falling, fell, fallen)

to drop downwards *My little brother is learning to walk but he keeps falling over.*

false

not true, correct or real *He gave a false name.*

family (families)

a group of people who are related to each other *There are nine people in their family.*

N O P Q R S T U V W X Y Z

famous
well-known *He's a famous singer*

fan
1 an object that you hold in your hand and move, or a machine that moves the air to make it cooler *Sit in front of the fan and relax.*
2 someone who likes a particular thing or person very much *My uncle is a Beatles fan.*

far (faraway)
not near, a distance away *I love getting letters from faraway places.*

farm
a place where people grow crops and raise animals *Cows are kept on dairy farms.*

▶ farm

fast
quick, not slow *Racing cars are very fast.*

fat
1 weighing more than is good or normal *It isn't healthy to be too fat.*
2 thick, big or wide *Our teacher reads to us from a big, fat book.*

father
a male parent *Dad reads to me at night.*

favourite
liked the best *Blue is my favourite colour.*

fax (faxes)

1 a document sent by fax *There's a fax for you.*
2 a machine that you use to send documents down a telephone line *Use the fax to send a message.*

fear (fearing, feared)

to have the feeling that something bad is going to happen or has happened *There is nothing to fear!*

feast

a large, special meal to celebrate something *Christmas dinner is a feast at our house.*

feather

one of the soft, light things that cover a bird's body *Peacock feathers are beautiful colours.*

▲ feather

feed (feeding, fed)

to give food to a person or an animal *It's fun to feed the chickens.*

◀ feed

feel (feeling, felt)

1 to have an emotion *I feel happy!*
2 to touch or be touched by something *This sweater feels rough.*

female

a woman, girl or animal that can have babies when adult *Female sheep are called ewes.*

fence

a wall made of wood or wire *There are plants growing up our garden fence.*

N O P Q R S T U V W X Y Z

ferry (ferries)

a kind of ship
*The ferry
leaves at
noon.*

▶ ferry

few

1 not many *There are few tickets left.*
2 a small number *I have a few friends.*

field

a piece of land for growing crops,
raising animals or playing sports
There is a bull in that field.

fierce

angry and strong, or violent *Guard
dogs can be very fierce.*

fight

when two or more people try to
hurt each other *I must stop the fight.*

figure

1 a written number *Write all the
figures down.*
2 a person's shape *She saw the figure
of a woman in the shadows.*

file

1 information on a computer *Move
your files to a new folder.*
2 information about a person or
subject kept for a reason *The doctor
has files on all of the patients.*

fill (filling, filled)

to put things into something until it
is full *Fill the vase with water before
putting the flowers in.*

film

1 thin plastic that you put into a
camera to take photographs *Digital
cameras don't use film.*
2 a movie *We saw the film at the
cinema.*

A B C D E **F** G H I J K L M

·Puzzle time·

What's the missing letter?

fin_sh   f_ght
f_eld   f_erce

answer:
finish fight field fierce

find (finding, found)
to see or get something that you are looking for *Can you find the answer?*

fine
1 very thin or in small pieces *The beach is covered with fine, white sand.*
2 very good *They are fine singers.*

finger
one of the five long parts on your hand *Your thumb is a finger.*

finish (finishing, finished)
to end *Put your pencil down when you have finished.*

fire
something that burns, giving out heat and flames *We sat around the fire.*

fire engine
a truck used to put out fires *Fire engines have flashing lights.*

firework
small objects that explode into bright colours in the sky *The fireworks start after dark.*

▶ fish

fish
an animal that lives in water, has fins and breathes through gills *There are seven fish in the tank.*

N O P Q R S T U V W X Y Z

fist
a closed hand *Which fist is the coin in?*

fit
to look and feel healthy *I feel very fit.*

fix (fixing, fixed)
1 to mend, to repair *I can fix the car.*
2 to stick or attach *Fix the picture to the wall.*

flag
a piece of cloth that is used as a signal, or the sign of a country *Stars and stripes are on the flag of the USA.*

▲ flag

flame
burning gas from a fire, or bright light from a candle *The flame is hot!*

flash
a burst of light *The light flashed on.*

flat
1 a room or rooms in a bigger building *My uncle lives in a flat.*
2 not bumpy or hilly, smooth *It's a very flat country.*

flavour
the taste of something *Chocolate and vanilla are flavours of ice cream.*

·Puzzle time·

Can you guess these flavours?
1. v_nilla   2. choc_l_te
3. str_wberr_   4. ban_n_

answers: 1. vanilla 2. chocolate
3. strawberry 4. banana

flight
a journey in a plane *It's a night flight.*

float (floating, floated)
not to sink *Float in the pool.*

A B C D E F G H I J K L M

flood
a lot of water in a place that is usually dry *There were heavy rains and then a flood.*

floor
part of a building that you stand on *Everyone is sitting on the floor.*

petal ▼ flower
stamen
stem

flower
the part of a plant that makes the seeds or fruit *Roses, pansies, and daisies are all flowers.*

fly (flying, flew)
1 to move through the air *We flew at night.*
2 a small insect *A fly buzzed by me.*

fog
mist or cloud *You can't see far in fog.*

fold (folding, folded)
to turn or bend something over on itself *Fold your clothes.*

follow (following, followed)
to move after or behind someone or something *Follow me!*

food
something that people or animals eat *This food tastes delicious.*

foolish
silly *It is a foolish idea.*

foot (feet)
the part of your body at the end of your leg that you stand and walk on *My father has very big feet.*

football
a game that is played by two teams who try to kick a ball into a net to score goals *We play football every day.*

N O P Q R S T U V W X Y Z

forget (forgetting, forgotten)
to not remember something *Don't forget to do your homework.*

fork
1 something with a handle and two or more points that is used for eating *The fork goes to the left of the plate.*
2 a tool used for digging *Turn the soil with a fork.*
3 the place in a road or river that divides in two *The road forks here.*

▲ How many things can you see beginning with 'f'?

forwards
towards the front *Take a step forwards.*

fossil
the print of an animal or plant that lived long ago *Fossils show us what life was like millions of years ago.*

fountain
a jet of water that is pushed up into the air *There is a fountain in the city centre.*

▶ fox

fox (foxes)
a wild animal that looks like a dog with a bushy tail *Baby foxes are called cubs.*

fraction
a part of something *One-half, one-third and one-quarter are fractions.*

frame
the thing that fits around a door, window or picture *Frames can be wood or metal.*

A B C D E F G H I J K L M

freckle
a small, reddish-brown spot on a person's skin *I have freckles on my face.*

free
1 not controlled *Wednesday afternoon is free time at our school.*
2 not costing anything *The Internet is free for schools until 6:30 p.m.*

freeze (freezing, froze, frozen)
to turn to ice because the temperature is very cold *Water freezes at 0°C.*

fresh
1 just picked, grown or made *Fresh fruits and vegetables are healthy foods.*
2 clean and pure *Go and get some fresh air.*

friend
a person you know and like *Good friends are very special.*

friendly
kind and easy to get on with *We have very friendly neighbours.*

frighten (frightening, frightened)
to scare, to make afraid *Storms may frighten animals.*

▶ frog

frog
an animal with long legs that lives on land and in water *There are frogs in the pond.*

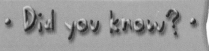

· Did you know? ·

Almost any frog can jump 20 times its own length.

front
the part of something that is the most forward *I sit at the front of class.*

N O P Q R S T U V W X Y Z

frost
white, icy powder that forms when it is very cold outside *The trees are covered in frost.*

frown (frowning, frowned)
to have a sad, angry or worried look on your face *Try not to frown.*

fruit
part of a plant that has seeds, such as an apple or grapes *I love fruit!*

▲ fruit

fry (frying, fried)
to cook something using oil *Fry the fish until it is cooked.*

full
containing as much as possible *Is the tank full yet?*

fun
enjoyable *This website is really fun.*

funny
making you laugh *The puppy is very funny.*

▼ fur

fur (furry)
soft, thick hair on the skin of an animal *The kitten has soft, fluffy fur.*

furniture
things such as chairs, tables, beds and desks *We have some new furniture.*

future
the time after now *In the future, we will have computers in our clothes.*

fuzzy
1 not clear *These pictures are fuzzy.*
2 curly and soft *My hair is fuzzy.*

Gg

gallop (galloping, galloped)

how animals such as horses or zebras run *The zebras galloped away.*

game

an activity that has rules *Let's play a board game.*

garage

1 a place to keep a car *The garage is next to the house.*
2 a place where cars are repaired *The car is at the garage.*

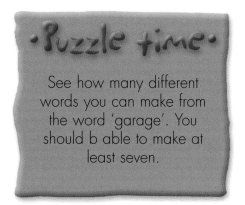

·Puzzle time·

See how many different words you can make from the word 'garage'. You should b able to make at least seven.

garden

land where flowers and plants can be grown *The garden is full of flowers.*

◀ garden

gate

a door in a fence or wall *There is a gate between our garden and our neighbour's.*

gentle

1 kind and careful not to hurt or disturb people or things *She is gentle with the animals.*
2 not loud or strong *There is a gentle breeze blowing.*

N O P Q R S T U V W X Y Z

geography
the study of countries *I like geography because we read about people and places.*

ghost
a dead person's spirit *Do you believe in ghosts?*

giant
an imaginary person who is very big *The story is about a giant.*

▶ giant

gift
something given to someone, a present *That's a lovely gift, thank you.*

giraffe
a very tall wild animal with a long neck *Giraffes live in Africa.*

girl
a female child *There are 15 girls in our class.*

give (gave, given)
1 to let someone have something *We gave our teacher a present.*
2 to pass something to someone *Give this cup to your sister.*

glad
happy about something *We're so glad you could come.*

glass
1 hard, clear material that is used to make windows, bottles and mirrors *The fish live in a glass bowl.*
2 a container for drinking from *I have a glass of water next to my bed.*

·Puzzle time·

Which of these objects is the odd one out ?

glass

bottle

jar

plate

answer: plate

glasses
two pieces of glass or plastic that you wear to protect your eyes or to see better *I wear glasses for reading.*

gloomy
1 dark *It's a gloomy day.*
2 sad *Don't look so gloomy, smile!*

glove
a piece of clothing to wear on your hands *Where are your gloves?*

▼ gloves

glue (gluing, glued)
to stick things together *Glue the corners first.*

goal
1 the posts in a game such as football or hockey, where the player tries to place the ball *The goalkeeper is a very important player.*
2 the point given to a team when it puts the ball inside the goal *That's another goal for our team.*
3 something you hope to do *My goal is to be a teacher.*

▶ goat

goat
a farm animal that usually has horns *Goats will eat almost anything.*

N O P Q R S T U V W X Y Z

gold
1 a valuable, yellow metal *The ring is made of gold.*
2 the colour of this metal *The present is wrapped up in gold paper.*

▶ gorilla

good (better, best)
1 of high quality *It's a very good school.*
2 pleasant *I'm having a good time.*
3 well-behaved *They have been really good children.*

goodbye (bye)
something you say when you are leaving someone *Goodbye and good luck!*

goose (geese)
a bird that looks like a big duck *There are geese on the farm.*

goosebumps
little bumps on your skin that appear when you are cold or frightened *The spooky story gave me goosebumps.*

gorilla
the biggest kind of ape *She studies gorillas.*

Did you know?

Gorillas were relatively unknown animals until the mid 1800s. In fact none were kept in zoos until 1911, in the United States.

grandparents (grandfather, grandmother)
the parents of your mother or father *Our grandparents live with us.*

grape

a small, round, juicy fruit that grows in bunches *Grapes can be red, green or purple.*

▶ grapes

grass

a green plant with thin leaves that grows over the ground *My brother is cutting the grass.*

gravity

the force that pulls things towards Earth and other planets *Gravity is what makes things fall to the ground.*

great

1 very good *This is a great song.*
2 very large *There was a great storm.*

greedy

wanting or taking more than is necessary *He was a greedy king.*

ground

1 the surface of the Earth that is under your feet *Lie on the ground and look up at the stars.*
2 the soil on and under the surface of the Earth *We are digging a hole in the ground near the pond.*
3 land used for a purpose *The football ground is on the edge of town.*

group

people or things that are together or connected *A group of us are playing in the paddling pool.*

▼ group

grow (growing, grew, grown)

to become larger or longer *The flowers are growing very well.*

N O P Q R S T U V W X Y Z

guard (guarding, guarded)
to protect someone or something
There is a guard outside.

guess (guessing, guessed)
to try to give the right answer when
you are not sure if it is correct
Guess which hand it is in.

▶ guinea pig

guinea pig
a furry animal with no tail that
people keep as a pet *We have a guinea
pig in our classroom.*

▲ How many things can you see
beginning with 'g'?

guitar
a stringed musical
instrument with a long
neck *He plays the guitar
in a band.*

◀ guitar

gun
a weapon that fires bullets *Guns are
dangerous weapons.*

gym
a place where people go to exercise
*There are lots of different machines at
the gym.*

A B C D E F **G** **H** I J K L M

Hh

hair
thin threads that grow on your skin and head *She has long, brown hair.*

half (halves)
one of two equal parts *Would you like half an apple?*

ham
meat from a pig's leg *Some ham tastes salty.*

hamburger
minced beef cooked and served in a round bun *I can make hamburgers.*

hammer
a tool used for hitting nails into wood *Use a hammer to bang the nail.*

▶ hammer

▶ hamster

hamster
a small, furry animal like a mouse. *Hamsters keep food in their cheeks.*

hand
the part of your body at the end of your arm *Your fingers and thumb are attached to your hand.*

handbag
a bag used for keeping things in *Mum keeps a hair brush and keys in her handbag.*

handsome
nice-looking *He's a very handsome man.*

N O P Q R S T U V W X Y Z

hang (hanging, hanged, hung)
to attach the top part of something, leaving the lower part free or loose *Sam hung on to the branch.*

happen (happening, happened)
to be, to take place *Who knows what will happen?*

happy
feeling pleased *This is a happy day.*

▲ happy

harbour
a safe place for ships and boats near land *The fishing boats leave the harbour early in the morning.*

hard
1 not soft *This bed is very hard.*
2 difficult, not easy *The questions are very hard.*

hat
a piece of clothing that you wear on your head *You must wear a hat in the sun.*

hate (hating, hated)
to strongly dislike something or someone *Our cat hates going to the vet for her injections.*

head
1 the part of your body above your neck *Put your hands on your head.*
2 a person who is the leader *The head of the school is in charge.*

healthy
well and strong *Our new baby is a healthy girl.*

hear (hearing, heard)
1 to be aware of sounds by using your ears *Can you hear the rain?*
2 to get news or be told something *I hear you're moving away.*

heart
1 the part of your body that pumps your blood *Your heart beats faster when you run.*
2 the main part of something *It's in the heart of the city.*
3 a shape that means love *Valentine cards are decorated with hearts.*

heat (heating, heated)
to make something warm *Heat the soup but don't boil it.*

heavy
weighing a lot *These books are heavy.*

hedgehog
a small, wild animal with sharp hairs on its back *Hedgehogs like milk.*

▼ heart

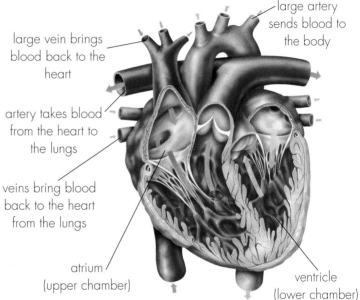

large vein brings blood back to the heart

large artery sends blood to the body

artery takes blood from the heart to the lungs

veins bring blood back to the heart from the lungs

atrium (upper chamber)

ventricle (lower chamber)

heel
1 the back part of your foot *Your heel is under your ankle.*
2 the part of a shoe that is under your heel *Mum's shoes have high heels.*

N O P Q R S T U V W X Y Z

height
how tall something is *What is your height in centimetres?*

▶ helicopter

helicopter
an aircraft with blades on top that spin and make it fly *Helicopters can land in smaller spaces than planes.*

hello
what you say when you see or meet someone, or when you answer the telephone *Hello! How are you?*

▶ helmet

helmet
a hat that protects your head *Always wear a helmet when you ride your bike.*

help (helping, helped)
to make it easier for someone to do something *Let me help you.*

hen
female chicken *Hens lay eggs.*

here
in this place *I like it here.*

hibernate (hibernating, hibernated)
to sleep during cold weather *Some animals hibernate in winter.*

hide (hiding, hid, hidden)
to put yourself or something out of sight *Hide the presents, she's coming.*

high
1 a long way from the bottom to the top *The mountain is very high.*
2 a long way above *The plane is high above us.*

A B C D E F G H I J K L M

hill
ground that is raised *Run down the hill.*

▶ hill

hippopotamus (hippopotamuses, hippopotami)
a large animal that lives near rivers and lakes in Africa *Hippopotamuses leave the water at night to eat grass.*

history
things that have happened in the past *Our town history is very interesting.*

hit (hitting, hit)
to swing your hand or something you are holding against something else *Hit the ball as hard as you can.*

hobby (hobbies)
something that you enjoy doing in your spare time *My hobbies are skateboarding and listening to music.*

▶ hobby

hockey
a game played by hitting a ball using wooden sticks *Hockey is a very fast game.*

hold (holding, held)
to have something in your hands or arms *Hold my coat, please.*

hole
an opening or an empty space *There's a hole in the bag.*

N O P Q R S T U V W X Y Z

holiday
1 a special day *It is a religious holiday.*
2 a time when you do not have to work or go to school *School holidays start soon.*

hollow
empty inside *The log is hollow.*

hologram
a picture made with a laser *There is a hologram on the sticker.*

home
the place where you live *What time will you get home?*

homework
school work you do at home *I do my homework when I get home from school.*

honey
a sweet, sticky food made by bees *Put honey in your yoghurt.*

▶ hood

hood
a piece of clothing that covers your head, usually attached to a coat or jacket *Put your hood up, it's raining.*

hoof (hooves)
the foot of an animal, such as a deer, horse or goat *Horses have very thick hooves.*

hook
a piece of metal or plastic for hanging up or catching things *Hang your jacket on the hook.*

A B C D E F G **H** I J K L M

hoop

a large ring of metal, wood or plastic *It's fun to play with hoops.*

▲ hoops

hop (hopping, hopped)

to jump on one foot, or make a small jump with two feet *Can you hop on one foot?*

hope (hoping, hoped)

to wish for something *I hope you have a good time.*

horn

1 one of the hard, pointed things on an animal's head *Goats have horns.*
2 something that you push to make a noise *The horn is very loud.*

▲ horn

horrible

bad or unpleasant *What a horrible colour.*

horse

a large animal with four legs, a mane and a tail *My brother can ride a horse.*

▶ horse

N O P Q R S T U V W X Y Z

hospital
the place where sick or injured people go to get better *Have you ever stayed in hospital?*

hot
at a very high temperature *Mercury is the hottest planet in the Solar System.*

▲ How many things can you see beginning with 'h'?

hot dog
a sausage in a long bun *Would you like a hot dog?*

hotel
a place people pay to stay in. *There's a hotel on the beach.*

hour
sixty minutes *It will take at least an hour for us to get to work.*

house
a building that people live in *My best friend lives in the house across the street from me.*

huge
very big *There is a huge crowd waiting outside.*

human (human being)
a person, not an animal *Humans are very intelligent.*

hump
a large bump *Some camels have two humps and others have just one.*

hungry
feeling that you need food *I'm hungry. What's for dinner?*

A B C D E F G **H** I J K L M

hunt (hunting, hunted)
1 to look for something or someone *We hunted everywhere for the other shoe.*
2 to try to catch wild animals *The owl hunted for mice at night.*

▶ hunt

· *Did you know?* ·

When hunting, owls use sharp claws called talons to grab their prey.

hurricane
a very strong wind storm *Hurricanes can cause lots of damage.*

hurry (hurrying, hurried)
to do something quickly *Hurry and get your coat.*

hurt (hurting, hurt)
1 to cause pain or harm *The dentist won't hurt you.*
2 to feel pain *My knee hurts.*

husband
the man who a woman is married to *Dad is Mum's husband.*

▼ hurricane

N O P Q R S T U V W X Y Z

ice

water that is so cold that it has frozen and become hard *Do you want ice in your water?*

◀ ice

iceberg

a large piece of ice that floats in the sea *We saw the tip of an iceberg.*

> • **Did you know?** •
>
> Almost 90 percent of an iceberg is below the surface of the water.

ice cream

a frozen, sweet food that is usually made of milk or cream *Ice cream tastes good on hot days.*

ice skate (ice skating, ice skated)

to move across ice wearing boots with a metal blade on the bottom *We're learning how to ice skate.*

▼ icing

icing

a sweet covering for cakes *Spread the icing evenly around the cake.*

idea

a plan or a thought about how to do something *Have you any ideas about how we can raise money for the school outing?*

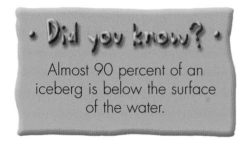

◀ ice cream

igloo
an Inuit house made of blocks of snow and ice *Inuit people live in igloos in winter.*

ill
not well, sick *He's feeling quite ill.*

imaginary
not real *The story is about an imaginary cat with special powers.*

imitate (imitating, imitated)
to copy *I can imitate the way you talk.*

immediately
now, at once, right away *Please put your clothes away immediately.*

important
1 serious, useful or valuable *It is a very important discovery.*
2 powerful *The mayor is an important person in our town.*

impossible
not able to be, be done or to happen *That's impossible – you can't be in two places at once!*

information
facts or knowledge about someone or something *There is a lot of information on our website.*

How many things can you see beginning with 'i'?

initial
the first letter of a person's name *What is your middle initial?*

injection
a way of putting medicine into your body using a special needle *The nurse at our school gives injections.*

N O P Q R S T U V W X Y Z

injure (injuring, injured)
to hurt or harm yourself or someone else *Luckily, no one was injured in the crash.*

ink
coloured liquid that is used for writing, drawing or printing *Sign your name in ink.*

▲ insect

insect
a small animal with six legs, wings and a body that has three parts *Beetles, butterflies and bees are all kinds of insects.*

•Puzzle time•

Can you find three insects hidden in this wordsearch?

t r b e e o
s d l e f w
e u a y a a
c a n d d s
a e t r o p
z x c t n o

answers: ant bee wasp

inside
in or into a place or container *Come inside the house, it's very cold out there.*

A B C D E F G H I J K L M

instrument
something people use to do a job
We use instruments to make music.

triangle

tambourine

guitar

drum

▶ instruments

interested
wanting to pay attention to
something or someone so that
you can learn more *Sam is interested
in sport.*

interesting
exciting in a way that keeps your
attention *Emailing children in other
countries is really interesting.*

Internet
a huge system of linked computers
all over the world that lets
people communicate with
each other *We use the
Internet at home and at
school.*

**interrupt,
interrupting, interrupted)**
to break in or stop someone
who is doing something or
saying something *The phone
call interrupted our conversation.*

invade (invading, invaded)
to attack or go into a place in
large numbers *The Vikings left their
ships and invaded the land.*

invent (inventing, invented)
to make something that has not
been made before *Computers were
invented about 65 years ago.*

N O P Q R S T U V W X Y Z

invention

something new that someone makes, or produces, for the first time *The telephone is the invention of Alexander Graham Bell.*

inventions ▽

telephone (1876)

car (1885)

flying machine (1874)

invisible

not possible to see *You can't read it, it is written in invisible ink!*

invite (inviting, invited)

to ask someone if they would like to do something such as come to a party *Ellie always invites lots of people to her parties.*

invitation

a note or a card that asks you to go to a party *Have you replied to your party invitation?*

iron

1 a strong, hard metal *The machinery is made from iron.*
2 a machine for smoothing clothes *Be careful, the iron gets very hot.*

island

a piece of land that has water all around it *There are thousands of islands in the Pacific Ocean.*

▶ island

A B C D E F G H I J K L M

Jj

jacket

a piece of clothing that look like a short coat *You should take a jacket with you.*

◀ jacket

jail (or gaol)

a prison, a place where people are kept by the police *The thief was put in jail for seven months.*

jam

a sweet food made from fruit *We have toast and jam for breakfast.*

jar

a glass container for storing food *Jam and honey are sold in jars.*

jealous

feeling angry or bad because you want something that someone else has *He is jealous of our grades.*

jeans

trousers made of denim *My favourite clothes are jeans and a t-shirt.*

▶ jeans

jeep

an open vehicle that is used for driving over rough ground *It was a bumpy ride in the jeep.*

jelly

a clear, sweet solid food made from fruit juice *We have ice cream and jelly at birthday parties.*

N O P Q R S T U V W X Y Z

jellyfish

a sea animal that floats on the surface and can sting *There are many different types of jellyfish.*

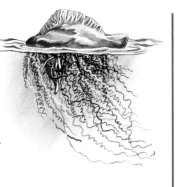

▲ jellyfish

jet

a fast aeroplane *There are several jet fighters in the air show.*

▲ jets

jewel

a kind of stone that is extremely valuable, such as diamonds, sapphires or rubies *The crown was covered in beautiful jewels.*

jewellery

things such as necklaces, bracelets and earrings that you wear for decoration *She wore jewellery to the party.*

▲ jewellery

jigsaw

a puzzle made from shaped pieces that fit together to make a picture *The jigsaw has 100 pieces.*

▶ jigsaw

job

work that you get paid for doing *She has a new job.*

A B C D E F G H I J K L M

join (joining, joined)

1 to become a member of a club or other group *I've joined the chess club.*
2 to stick or fasten together *Join the two pieces of card.*

joke

a funny story that is told to make people laugh *Do you know any jokes?*

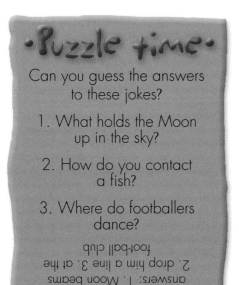

·Puzzle time·

Can you guess the answers to these jokes?

1. What holds the Moon up in the sky?

2. How do you contact a fish?

3. Where do footballers dance?

answers: 1. Moon beams 2. drop him a line 3. at the football club

jolly

happy *He's a jolly person.*

journey

a trip or the distance travelled *We were very tired after the long journey.*

judo

a Japanese fighting sport *In judo, people try to throw each other to the floor.*

jug

a container for liquids *Fill the jug with water.*

▶ juice

juice

liquid from fruit or vegetables *You can have orange juice or apple juice.*

N O P Q R S T U V W X Y Z

jump
(jumping, jumped)

to push yourself off the ground with both feet *Jump as high as you can.*

▲ jump

jumper

a piece of clothing that covers your upper body that you pull over your head *That looks like a nice, warm jumper.*

jungle

a thick forest in a hot country *The trees and plants in a jungle grow very close together.*

▶ jungle

How many things can you see beginning with 'j'?

just

1 to have happened a very short time ago *I've only just arrived home from work.*
2 the right amount or thing *There was just enough flour to make a cake.*
3 only *Don't worry about the new job, it's just a temporary position.*

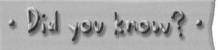

Did you know?

More kinds of animals and plants live in jungles than any other area of the world.

A B C D E F G H I J K L M

kk

kaleidoscope

a tube with pictures or pieces of coloured glass or plastic at one end that you look through and turn to see changing patterns *The kaleidoscope was invented in 1816.*

▶ kaleidoscope

kangaroo

an Australian animal that keeps its young in a pouch on the front of its body *Kangaroos have big, strong back legs.*

karate

a Japanese fighting sport *In karate, you fight using your hands and feet.*

▶ karate

keep (keeping, kept)

1 to continue to have something *You can keep the books for two weeks.*
2 to continue to do something *Don't keep staring at that man.*
3 to have something in a certain place *The paints are kept in a cupboard.*

kettle

a container or machine for boiling water *Come in, I'll put the kettle on and make some tea.*

key

1 a piece of metal used to open a lock *Have you seen my front door key?*
2 one of the parts of a computer or piano that you press with your fingers *Type the file name and then press the 'enter' key.*
3 a set of answers or an explanation of symbols *There is a key at the back of the book.*

N O P Q R S T U V W X Y Z

keyboard

the set of keys on a computer or a piano that you press to type or make a sound *This is a special keyboard with letters and pictures.*

kick (kicking, kicked)

to swing your foot at something *Kick the ball into the goal!*

▲ kick

kill (killing, killed)

to cause someone or something to die *Some weeds kill other plants.*

kind

helpful, pleasant and thoughtful *It's very kind of you to think of me.*

king

a royal man who rules a country *Do you think the prince will become king?*

◀ king

• **Did you know?** •

Henry VIII (eighth) was king of England from 1509 to 1547. He had six wives.

kiss (kissing, kissed)

to touch someone else with your lips *Mum kissed us all goodnight.*

A B C D E F G H I J **K** L M

kitchen

the room in a house for preparing food *There are nice smells coming from the kitchen.*

•Puzzle time•

How many kitchen things can you find in this word puzzle?

sinkovencupboardtable chairshelfcupandsaucer

answer: there are eight things – sink oven cupboard table chair shelf cup saucer

kite

a toy made of light wood and cloth, paper or plastic, flown at the end of some string *Shall we fly the kite today?*

kitten

a baby cat *Our cat has had a litter of kittens.*

▶ kittens

knee

the part of your leg that bends *When you walk, you bend your knees.*

kneel (kneeling, knelt)

to get down on your knees *Dad knelt down to stroke the cat.*

How many things can you see beginning with 'k'?

N O P Q R S T U V W X Y Z

knife

a tool with a blade for cutting things into pieces *Put the knife to the right of your plate.*

knight

a kind of soldier who lived hundreds of years ago *Knights wore armour when they rode into battle.*

knit (knitting, knitted)

to join wool together with long metal sticks *Jodie can knit.*

▲ knitting

knock (knocking, knocked)

to hit something to make a noise *Knock on the back door.*

▲ knot

knot

the place where two pieces of string or rope are tied together *There are many different ways that you can tie a knot.*

know

1 to have information or knowledge in your mind *I know that there are nine planets in our Solar System.*
2 to have met someone before or be familiar with them *I know Mrs Smith really well.*

A B C D E F G H I J **K** **L** M

Ll

label
a piece of paper or cloth that gives information about the thing it is attached to *Always put a label on your floppy disks.*

lace
fine cloth made with patterns of tiny holes *The doll's dress is made of lace.*

ladder
a piece of equipment made from two long bars joined together by short bars, which is used for climbing up to reach high places *Dad uses a ladder when he paints the house.*

ladybird
an insect that is red with black spots *Ladybirds are good for the garden.*

▶ ladybird

lake
a big area of water that has land all around it *The lake has frozen.*

▶ lamb

lamb
a young sheep or the meat from that animal *Lambs are born in the spring.*

lamp
a machine that gives light *Switch on the lamp, it's too dark to see.*

land
1 ground *We bought a plot of land.*
2 the dry part of the Earth *The sailors were very happy to see land.*
3 a place or a country *The castle is in a magical land far away.*

land (landing, landed)
to reach the ground after being in the air *The plane lands at 2:45 p.m.*

N O P Q R S T U V W X Y Z

language

words people use to communicate
Our teacher speaks two languages.

How many things can you see
beginning with 'l'?

lap

1 the top of your legs when you are
sitting down *My cat sits on my lap.*
2 once around a track *They ran
12 laps of the track.*

large

big *We ate a large piece of cake.*

laser

a powerful light or the machine that
makes it *We saw a brilliant laser show
at the museum.*

last

1 after the others *We came last in the
egg and spoon race.*
2 the one that happened the shortest
time ago *We went to Italy for our last
holiday.*

last (lasting, lasted)

to continue to work or to be *How
long do you think this good weather
will last?*

late

1 after the normal or correct time
Sorry I'm late!
2 towards the end of a period of
time *It was late on Sunday afternoon
when we left for town.*

laugh (laughing, laughed)

to make a sound that shows you
are happy, or when you think
something is funny *We laughed at
Dad's silly joke.*

A B C D E F G H I J K L M

law
a rule made by the government
A new law has been passed.

lawn
a place in a garden or a park that is covered in grass that is cut short
Mow the lawn.

lay (laying, laid)
1 to put in a place *Lay the coats over the back of the chair.*
2 to make an egg *The hens lay an egg most days.*

lazy
1 a name given to someone who doesn't like work *She's the laziest girl in the class.*
2 not busy, relaxed *We had a nice, lazy weekend.*

lead (leading, led)
1 to show someone the way *The dog led them to the children.*
2 to be in the front *The champion is leading the parade.*

lean (leaning, leant, leaned)
1 to be in or move into a position that is not straight *Lean over the fence and pick up the ball.*
2 to rest against something *Chris was leaning against the wall, watching the match.*

leap (leaping, leapt)
to jump into the air or over something *The frog leapt into the pond.*

◀ leap

N O P Q R S T U V W X Y Z

learn (learning, learnt, learned)
to get knowledge or information about a subject *We are learning to paint pictures at school.*

leave (leaving, left)
1 to go away from a place *What time are you leaving?*
2 to put a thing in a place or to let a thing stay in a place *You can leave your bike in the garden.*

leg
1 the part of your body that you stand up with, between your hip and your foot *Dad's legs are a lot longer than mine are.*
2 the part of a table or chair that holds it up *One of the chair legs is broken.*

lemon
a sour yellow fruit *We put lemon juice and sugar on the pancakes.*

lend (lending, lent)
to let someone have or use something that they will return after using *Lend me a pen, please.*

leopard
a large cat with yellow or white fur and black spots *Leopards are beautiful animals.*

◀ leopard

leotard
a stretchy piece of clothing that you wear for dancing or exercising *We wear leotards in ballet class.*

lesson
a time in which someone is taught something such as a skill or a subject *I go to extra French lessons every Thursday after school.*

A B C D E F G H I J K **L** M

let (letting, let)
1 to allow someone to do something *Will your mum let you sleep over tonight?*
2 to allow something to happen *Just let the ball fall.*

letter
1 one of the signs of the alphabet used in writing *There are five letters in James' name.*
2 a written message that you put in an envelope and send or give someone *You can either send a letter or an email.*

lettuce
a green, leafy vegetable eaten in salads *We're growing lettuce this year.*

▶ lettuce

library
a place where books are kept *A mobile library comes to our village twice a week.*

lick (licking, licked)
to put your tongue on something *Lick your ice cream, it's going to drip.*

lie (lying, lay, lain)
to have your body flat on the floor, ground or bed. *We put our towels on the sand and lay down.*

lie (lying, lied)
to say something that is not the truth *They lied about their age.*

life (lives)
1 the time between when you are born and when you die *He had a long, happy life.*
2 being alive *Do you think there is life on other planets?*

N O P Q R S T U V W X Y Z

lifeboat
a boat that helps people who are in danger at sea *The fishermen were rescued by the lifeboat just in time.*

lift
1 a machine that takes you up and down in a building *Take the lift to the fourth floor.*
2 a ride in a car *Do you need a lift?*

lift (lifting, lifted)
to move something to a higher place *It took four people to lift our piano.*

light
1 energy or brightness from the Sun or a lamp that lets you see things *Is there enough light to take a picture?*
2 a machine that makes light *Turn off the light, it's time for bed.*

lighthouse
a tower on the coast that has a bright light that flashes to warn ships *There's a lighthouse at the end of the beach.*

lightning
electrical light in the sky during a storm *We could see lightning in the distance.*

like (liking, liked)
1 to enjoy something or be fond of someone or something *I really like skateboarding.*
2 to want *What would you like for your birthday?*

prism

▶ light

light splits into the seven colours of the rainbow when it passes through a prism (glass triangle)

A B C D E F G H I J K L M

line
1 a long, thin mark *Draw a line through the mistakes.*
2 a piece of string, rope or wire *Hang the clothes on the line.*
3 a row *There is a line of trees as you go into the park.*

▶ lion

lion
a large wild cat *Lions live in Africa.*

lips
the edges of your mouth *The cat came in, licking his lips.*

liquid
something, such as water, that is not hard and can be poured *There's some liquid soap in the bathroom.*

listen (listening, listened)
to pay attention to sound *Sorry, what did you say? I wasn't listening.*

litter
1 rubbish lying on the ground *We picked up all the litter in the playground.*
2 the group of babies that an animal has at one time *Our dog had a litter of puppies last night.*

little
small, not large or not much *We gave the cat a little milk.*

live (living, lived)
1 to be alive *My great grandfather lived to be 80 years old.*
2 to have your home in a certain place *They live in France now.*

living room
a room in a house for sitting and relaxing in *The TV is in the living room.*

N O P Q R S T U V W X Y Z

lizard
a short, four-legged animal that lays eggs *Lizards are cold-blooded animals.*

loaf (loaves)
bread that is baked in one piece *Get a loaf of bread and some milk from the shop.*

lobster
a sea animal with eight legs and two claws *We saw a lobster through the glass bottom of the boat.*

▼ lobster

lock
an object that is used to close something, usually opened and shut with a key *There's a lock on the chest.*

lock (locking, locked)
to close or fasten something with a key *Have you locked the door?*

loft
the inside of the roof of a house *There's an old tennis racket in the loft.*

◀ lizard

log
a thick piece of a tree *It's cold in here, put another log on the fire.*

lonely
feeling sad that you are on your own *Come over if you get lonely.*

long
1 measuring a big distance from one end to the other *Is it a long walk?*
2 continuing for a large amount of time *It's a very long movie.*

look (looking, looked)
to pay attention to something that you see *Look at that hot air balloon.*

A B C D E F G H I J K L M

loose
1 not tight *Wear loose clothes.*
2 free to move *The lions were set loose.*

lose (losing, lost)
1 to not be able to find something *He keeps losing his glasses.*
2 to not win a competition or a game *Our team lost the competition.*

loud
not quiet, making a lot of noise *Turn the music down, that's too loud!*

love (loving, loved)
to like someone or something very much *We love our new baby.*

lovely
beautiful or pleasant *It's a lovely day.*

low
close to the ground, not high *There are some low clouds around the hills.*

lucky
1 fortunate, having good things happen to you *They're lucky they won.*
2 giving good luck *These are my lucky football boots.*

lunch
a meal that you eat in the middle of the day *Why don't we meet for lunch?*

▲ lunch

lungs
parts of your body inside your chest that help you to breathe *You have two lungs protected by bones called ribs.*

N O P Q R S T U V W X Y Z

Mm

machine

a piece of equipment that is used to do a job *Washing machines wash, rinse and spin your clothes.*

◀ machine

magic

a power to make strange things happen *I can do magic tricks.*

magnet

a piece of metal that makes some other metal objects move towards it *Use a magnet to pick up all the pins.*

main

the most important or the biggest *We'll meet you in front of the main entrance.*

make (making, made)

1 to create or build something *The computer was made in a factory.*
2 to cause something to happen or be a certain way *That joke always makes me laugh.*

male

a man, boy or an animal that cannot produce eggs or have babies *Male elephants are bigger than female elephants.*

mammal

the group of animals that give birth to live babies and make milk for them to drink *The elephant is the largest land mammal.*

◀ mammal

A B C D E F G H I J K L **M**

man (men)
an adult male *That is a men's shop.*

many
large in number *There are many good reasons to use the Internet.*

map
a drawing that shows where things are in a building, town, country or other place *We studied a map of the world.*

▶ marbles

marble
1 a type of hard stone *The walls are marble.*
2 a small glass or metal ball used to play a game *I won two marbles in that last game.*

march (marching, marched)
to walk with regular steps *The band marched at the front of the parade.*

mark
1 a sign or shape *Put a mark to show where your house is.*
2 a letter or number that a teacher puts on a piece of work to show how good it is *She's getting really good marks this term.*
3 a spot or a dark patch on something that makes it look bad *There is a mark on the carpet where we spilled the juice.*

market
a place where you can buy food, clothes, plants and other things *Most markets are outdoors.*

marmalade
jam that is made from oranges *We had toast and marmalade for breakfast.*

N O P Q R S T U V W X Y Z

marry (marrying, married)
to become husband and wife *They married three years ago.*

mask
something that you put over your face to hide or protect it *He always wore a mask.*

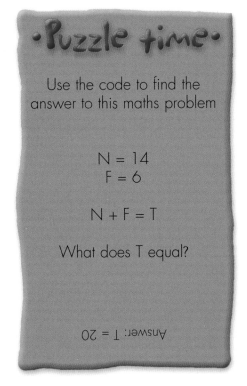

◀ mask

mat
a piece of material that covers a floor or table *Wipe your feet on the mat.*

match (matches)
1 a small stick that makes a flame when you rub it against something *We have special long matches for lighting the fire.*
2 a contest or game *That's the best football match I've ever seen.*

mathematics (maths)
the study of numbers or shapes *Mathematics is studied in schools.*

•Puzzle time•

Use the code to find the answer to this maths problem

$N = 14$
$F = 6$

$N + F = T$

What does T equal?

Answer: T = 20

meadow
a field with grass and flowers *The meadow was covered in pretty flowers.*

meal
a time when food is eaten or the actual food itself *Sometimes you feel sleepy after a big meal.*

mean
1 cruel or unkind *Don't be mean to each other.*
2 someone who does not want to spend money *The king is very mean – maybe that's why he's so rich.*

meaning
the information that is supposed to be understood from the use of words and signs *Can you explain the meaning of this sentence?*

measles
an illness that that can give you a high temperature and lots of red spots *When my little brother had measles, he had to stay in bed.*

measure (measures, measuring, measured)
to find out the size or amount of something *Measure each side of the room.*

meat
food made from animals *people who don't eat meat are called vegetarians.*

mechanic
a person who fixes cars and machines *He's a good mechanic.*

medal
a piece of metal that is given as a prize for winning a competition or for doing something special *He won a medal for bravery.*

◀ medal

N O P Q R S T U V W X Y Z

medicine

1 something that you take when you are not well so that you will get better *You have to take this medicine three times a day.*
2 the study of illness and injury *She is studying medicine.*

medium

a middle size between large and small *I'd like a medium popcorn, please.*

meet (meeting, met)

1 to know someone for the first time *We met the first day of school.*
2 to go to the same place as another person *Where shall we meet?*

melody (melodies)

a song or the tune of a song *The song has a strange but beautiful melody.*

melon

a fruit with a hard skin and flat seeds *Melons can be green, yellow or orange.*

melt (melting, melted)

to change from a solid to a liquid when heated *The ice in my drink has melted.*

◀ melt

memory (memories)

1 something that you remember from the past *Photographs bring back memories.*
2 the ability to remember things *Do you have a good memory?*
3 the part of a computer where information is stored *This computer has more memory than our old one.*

mend (mending, mended)

to repair *Could you help me mend the tyre?*

A B C D E F G H I J K L **M**

menu
1 the list of food in a café or restaurant *The waiter brought us each a menu.*
2 a list of things seen on a computer screen *Click here to go back to the main menu.*

message
information for a person from someone else *Leave a message for him on the note pad.*

messy
not tidy *This room is very messy.*

▲ How many things can you see beginning with 'm'?

metal
hard material such as gold, silver, copper or iron *Silver is a metal.*

microphone
something that is used for recording sounds or making them louder *Speak into the microphone.*

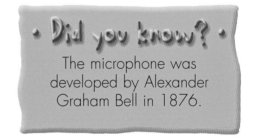

• **Did you know?** •
The microphone was developed by Alexander Graham Bell in 1876.

microscope
something that makes small things look much bigger *We looked at a hair under the microscope.*

microwave
an oven that cooks food very quickly using waves of electricity *Heat the soup in the microwave.*

N O P Q R S T U V W X Y Z

midday
12:00 in the middle of the day *We'll have our lunch early – at about midday.*

middle
the centre or the part of something that is between the beginning and the end *We sat down in the middle of the row.*

midnight
12:00 in the middle of the night *We stay up until midnight on New Year's Eve.*

▼ mirror

mild
1 not too strong or serious *She had a mild case of flu.*
2 not tasting too strong or too spicy *It's a mild curry.*
3 not too cold *The weather is mild today.*

milk
white liquid that female humans and other mammals produce to feed their babies *Milk is good for you.*

▶ milk

minus (minuses)
1 the sign used in maths when taking one number away from another *Twenty-five minus five equals twenty.*
2 in temperature, below zero *It's cold today, it's below minus one outside!*

minute
sixty seconds *We waited for twenty minutes but they didn't come.*

mirror
special glass that you can see your reflection or what's behind you in *Go and look in the mirror – you look really funny.*

A B C D E F G H I J K L **M**

miserable
very unhappy *Don't look so miserable.*

miss
not to hit a target *He missed the basket.*

mistake
something that is wrong *We all make mistakes.*

▶ mittens

mittens
gloves that do not have separate places for each finger *Wrap up well and wear your mittens.*

mix (mixing, mixed)
to put different things together *Mix the eggs and flour together.*

mobile phone
a small telephone that people can carry around *Call me on the mobile phone.*

model
1 a small copy of something such as a plane or a building *We made a model plane at the weekend.*
2 a person whose job is to show clothes *She wants to be a model.*
3 one type of something *This computer is the most up-to-date model.*

money
coins and paper that you use to buy things with *Have you spent all your money already?*

monitor
the part of a computer that shows the screen *It's easier to see on a big monitor.*

▼ monkey

monkey
an animal with a long tail that uses its legs to climb *We watched the monkeys at the zoo.*

N O P Q R S T U V W X Y Z

monster

a frightening creature in stories and films *The monster chased them into the forest.*

month

one of the twelve parts of the year *Months are 30 or 31 days long, except February.*

Moon

the small planet that travels around the Earth *The Moon is full tonight.*

more (most)

1 stronger or greater than *This book is more interesting.*
2 a larger or an additional amount or number *Is there any more cake?*

morning

the part of the day between the time the sun comes up and noon *We get up at the same time every morning.*

mosque

a building where Muslim people go to pray *The mosque is in the centre of the town.*

·Puzzle time·

Spot five differences between these two pictures

A B C D E F G H I J K L **M**
▲

moth
an insect that is similar to a butterfly *Moths are more active at night.*

mother
a woman who has a child or a female animal that has young *My mother is a nurse.*

motor
the part of a machine that uses power to make it work *There is a motor in the washing machine.*

motorbike (motorcycle)
a vehicle with two wheels and a seat for people to ride on *Dad has a new motorbike.*

▶ motorbike

mountain
land that has been pushed up very high *Some mountains have snow on top all year round.*

mouse (mice)
1 a small animal with a long tail and a pointed nose *There are mice in the field.*
2 the part of a computer with a ball in it that you move by hand to move things around on the screen *You can play this game using a mouse.*

▲ mouse

moustache
the hair that grows above a man's lip *He has a little moustache.*

mouth
the part of your face that you use to talk and eat *Don't talk with your mouth full.*

move (moving, moved)
to change the position of something *Could you move, I can't see the TV?*

N O P Q R S T U V W X Y Z

movie
a story that is told using pictures that move, a film *What movie would you like to see tonight?*

much
a lot *Thank you so much for coming.*

mud
wet soil or earth *I'm covered in mud!*

mug
a cup with tall sides *Do you want a mug of hot chocolate?*

multiply (multiplies, multiplying)
to add a number to itself, often more than once *two multiplied by two is four.*

munch (munches, munching, munched)
to eat something noisily *The rabbit munched on carrots and lettuce.*

muscle
one of the parts of the body that tightens and relaxes to cause movement *Relax your muscles.*

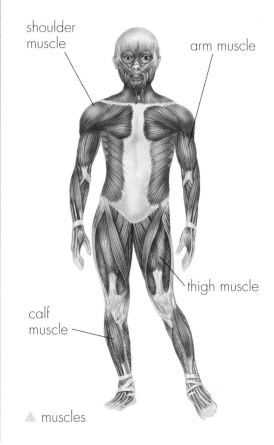

shoulder muscle

arm muscle

thigh muscle

calf muscle

▲ muscles

museum

a place where old, important, valuable or interesting things are kept so that people can go and look at them *There is a toy museum in our town.*

mushroom

a small vegetable that has a stem with a round top *Do you want mushrooms on your pizza?*

▶ mushrooms

music

a pattern of sounds that is sung or played on special instruments *Can you read music?*

▶ music

must

to have to do something *You must lock the door before going to bed at night.*

mysterious

something strange, secret or difficult to understand *He is a mysterious person, we don't know much about him.*

N O P Q R S T U V W X Y Z

Nn

nail

1 a thin, sharp piece of metal with one flat end that you hit with a hammer *Hang the picture on that nail.*

2 the hard covering on the ends of your fingers and toes *He bites his nails.*

▲ nails

name

what a person or object is called *What's your name?*

narrow

having only a short distance from one side to the other *The road is very narrow.*

nasty

very unpleasant or bad *That's a very nasty cut.*

nation

a country and the people who live there *It is a poor nation.*

naughty

badly behaved *Don't be naughty.*

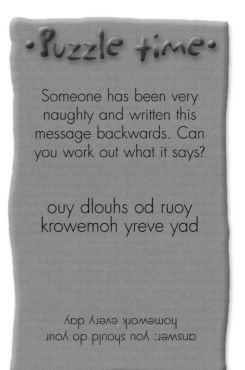

•Puzzle time•

Someone has been very naughty and written this message backwards. Can you work out what it says?

ouy dlouhs od ruoy krowemoh yreve yad

answer: you should do your homework every day

A B C D E F G H I J K L M

navy

the ships and people that fight for a country at sea during a war *My cousin is in the navy.*

near

close by, not far *There's a bus stop near the zoo.*

neat

1 clean or organised *His room is always neat and tidy.*
2 clearly presented *You have very neat handwriting.*

neck

the part of your body that attaches your head to your shoulders *Put a scarf around your neck.*

necklace

a piece of jewellery that you wear around your neck *That's a beautiful necklace.*

needle

1 a thin, sharp piece of metal with a hole through it used for sewing *First, thread the needle.*
2 a thin, sharp piece of metal through which injections are given *The needle will not hurt you.*

neighbour

a person who lives near another person *We invited all our friends and neighbours to the party.*

nephew

the son of your sister or brother *My nephew is staying with us for a few days.*

▶ necklace

N O P Q R S T U V W X Y Z

nervous

worried or frightened, not able to relax *She's a little nervous about being in the school play.*

▲ nest

nest

a place birds make to lay their eggs *There's a robin's nest in that tree.*

Did you know?

The weaver bird 'weaves' a complicated nest out of twigs and dry grass.

net

material that is made by joining pieces of string or thread together, leaving spaces between them *We use a small net when we go fishing.*

▲ net

network

a system of things or people that are connected *Link to a computer network.*

A B C D E F G H I J K L M

never

not at any time, not ever *I've never been to China.*

new

not old or used *I love your jacket, is it new?*

news

information about something that is happening now or that happened a short time ago *Write soon and send us all your news.*

newspaper

sheets of paper that are printed with words and pictures to tell you what is happening in the world *Have you read today's newspaper?*

next

the one that is nearest or immediately after another one *Who's next on the list?*

nice

enjoyable, good, pleasant *Did you have a nice time?*

niece

the daughter of your sister or brother *Her niece works in a bank.*

▲ night

night

the time of day between when the sun sets and rises again *The moon can be seen at night.*

nightgown (nightie)

a dress to sleep in *Put your nightgown on and get into bed.*

N O P Q R S T U V W X Y Z

nightmare
a bad dream *Nightmares can be very scary.*

nobody
no one, no person *There's nobody home.*

nod (nodding, nodded)
to quickly move your head up and down *She nodded her head in agreement with him.*

noise
loud sounds *Please keep the noise down, will you?*

noisy
very loud *There was noisy music coming from the concert hall.*

none
not any, not one *Sorry, there is none left in the box.*

nonsense
something that does not make any sense, or mean anything *The television programme was complete nonsense.*

noodles
very thin strips of food that are usually made from flour, water and eggs and then boiled *Do you want rice or noodles?*

▼ noodles

noon
midday, 12:00 *Shall we meet at noon tomorrow for lunch?*

A B C D E F G H I J K L M

no one
nobody, not one person *I have no one to talk to.*

normal
something that is ordinary or usual *It's normal to feel tired first thing in the morning.*

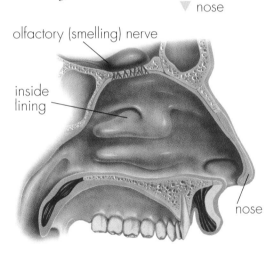

▼ nose

olfactory (smelling) nerve

inside lining

nose

nose
the part of your face that you use for breathing and smelling things *Breathe in deeply through your nose.*

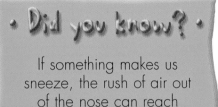

• Did you know? •

If something makes us sneeze, the rush of air out of the nose can reach speeds of 160 kilometres an hour!

note
1 a short written message *Mum wrote a note to the school.*
2 a piece of paper money *We paid with notes and coins.*
3 a musical sound or the mark to show a musical sound *The opera singer can hit very high notes.*

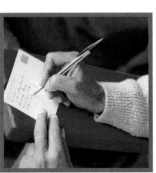

▶ note

N O P Q R S T U V W X Y Z

nothing

not anything, zero *There's nothing in the box, it's empty.*

notice (noticing, noticed)

1 to see something, or be aware that it is there *Did you notice if anyone was in the shop?*
2 a sign that tells people something *The notice says that the play starts tomorrow.*

novel

a long story in a book, which is written by an author *Have you read his latest novel?*

now

this time, the present *Where are you going now?*

nowhere

not anywhere *Your PE kit is nowhere to be found.*

number

1 a word or symbol that means the amount, quantity or order of something *Some people think seven is a lucky number.*
2 the numbers you press on a phone to call someone *What's your new number?*

▼ nurse

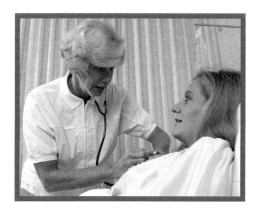

nurse

a person whose job is to take care of people who are sick or hurt *Go and see the school nurse, you don't look well.*

A B C D E F G H I J K L M

nursery (nurseries)

1 a place where small children are looked after during the day while their parents are at work *My little brother still goes to nursery.*

2 a place where plants are grown and sold *We bought some beautiful plants at the nursery on the hill.*

nursery rhyme

a poem or song usually written for young children *My favourite nursery rhymes are 'Jack and Jill', 'Baa Baa Black Sheep' and 'Humpty Dumpty'.*

▲ How many things can you see beginning with 'n'?

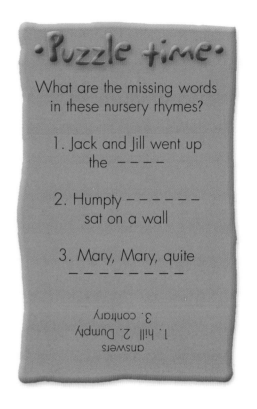

·Puzzle time·

What are the missing words in these nursery rhymes?

1. Jack and Jill went up the − − − −

2. Humpty − − − − − − sat on a wall

3. Mary, Mary, quite − − − − − − − −

answers
1. hill 2. Dumpty 3. contrary

nut

a seed that you can eat *Peanuts, cashews and almonds are all different types of nuts.*

N O P Q R S T U V W X Y Z

Oo

ocean

1 the salt water that covers most of the Earth *Strange fish live at the bottom of the ocean.*
2 a large sea *The Pacific Ocean is the largest ocean.*

· Did you know? ·

About 97 percent of all the water on Earth is in the oceans. The Pacific is the biggest and is twice as big as the next largest ocean, the Atlantic. This is followed by the Indian, Southern and Arctic Oceans.

octopus

a sea animal that has eight legs *The legs of the octopus are called tentacles.*

off

1 not on *Take the glass off the table.*
2 not in use or switched on *Shut the computer down before you switch it off.*
3 away from *Keep off the grass.*

office

a place where people work at desks *There are four people in my Mum's office.*

oil

1 a thick liquid made from plants or animals and used for cooking *Put a little olive oil in the pan.*
2 a thick liquid that comes out of the ground and is used to make petrol *They discovered oil there last year.*
3 a thick liquid that is used on metal or wood so that parts move better or more easily *This door is squeaking. Can you put some oil on it, please?*

◀ octopus

A B C D E F G H I J K L M

okay (OK)
1 fine, healthy, well *Are you okay?*
2 all right *Is it okay if I copy my work to your computer?*

old
not young, not new *My grandad is getting very old.*

◀ old

once
1 one time *We've met only once.*
2 one time in a fixed period *We go swimming once a week.*

▼ onions

onion
a vegetable that has a strong smell and taste *Do you want onion on your pizza?*

open
not closed or covered over *What time does the shop open?*

operation
when a doctor cuts open a person's body to mend or remove something *The operation took two hours.*

opposite
1 completely different *The opposite of near is far.*
2 across from, facing *They live in the house opposite.*

▶ orange

orange
a fruit that grows on trees and is the colour between red and yellow *Would you like some orange juice?*

N O P Q R S T U V W X Y Z

orbit (orbiting, orbited)
to travel round and round
something, like a planet in space
The Earth orbits the Sun.

orchestra
a group of people playing musical
instruments together *He plays violin
with the school orchestra.*

▲ How many things can you see
beginning with 'o'?

·Puzzle time·

Can you name all these
orchestral instruments?

1.

2.

3.

4.

answers
1. flute 2. drum 3. violin
4. cello

order
1 to ask for something in a
restaurant, shop or on the Internet
Can I order a coffee, please?
2 to tell someone what to do *The
captain ordered the men to attack the
ship.*

ordinary
not special, normal *It's just an
ordinary house.*

ostrich
a large, African bird with a long
neck *Ostriches cannot fly.*

A B C D E F G H I J K L M

otter

a brown, furry wild animal that swims and eats fish *Otters are rarely seen.*

▼ otter

out

1 not in *The mouse got out of his cage.*
2 not at home *She's out at the moment.*
3 out of – none left *We're out of sugar.*

outdoors

not inside a building, in the open air *It's much cooler outdoors.*

oven

something that you use to bake or roast food *Bake the cake in the oven for 45 minutes.*

over

1 above, covering *He put a blanket over us.*
2 finished, ended *Is the film over yet?*
3 from one side to another *A bridge runs over the river.*

owl

a bird that hunts at night *Sometimes you can hear an owl hooting.*

own (owning, owned)

to have something that you bought or were given *We own a new house.*

oxygen

a gas that animals and plants need to live *There is an oxygen mask above your seat.*

Pp

pack (packing, packed)
to put things into boxes, bags or suitcases *Don't forget to pack your suitcases.*

▶ pack

package
a small parcel *This package has your name on it.*

paddle (paddling, paddled)
1 to move a boat through water using oars or your hands *They paddled the canoe across the lake.*
2 to walk in shallow water *My little brother can't swim yet, but he likes to paddle.*

page
one side of a sheet of paper in a book, magazine or newspaper *This book has 128 pages.*

pain
the feeling you have when you are hurt or ill *I have a bad pain in my side.*

paint
a sticky liquid that you brush onto things to colour them *Don't spill paint on the carpet.*

▲ paint

pair
1 two things that go together *I need a new pair of trainers.*
2 something that is made of two similar things joined together *I've bought a new pair of sunglasses for my holiday.*

A B C D E F G H I J K L M

palace

a large, especially fine house where a king, queen or other important person lives *The palace is surrounded by beautiful gardens.*

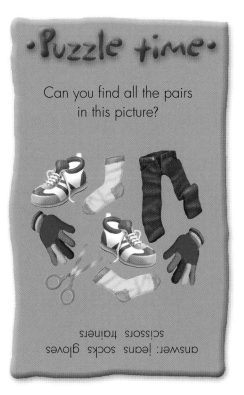

·Puzzle time·

Can you find all the pairs in this picture?

answer: jeans socks gloves scissors trainers

palm

1 the inside part of your hand *Fortune tellers read palms.*
2 a kind of tree with leaves only at the top *Our tent was under a row of palms on the beach.*

pan

a round cooking pot with a long handle *Melt the butter in a pan.*

pancake

a thin, flat cake that is cooked in a frying pan *I like pancakes with sugar.*

panda

a large, black and white animal that looks like a bear *Pandas come from China.*

pantomime

a funny musical show for children that is performed around Christmas *The pantomime is 'Robin Hood'.*

paper
1 thin sheets of material for writing or printing on *There is no paper in the printer.*
2 a newspaper *We recycle our newspapers once a week.*

parachute
a piece of equipment made of cloth that people wear to let them fall slowly through the air *The parachute will open automatically.*

parade
a number of people walking or marching in a long line to celebrate a special occasion *There is a parade every year.*

◀ parade

parent
a mother or father *We're making a special dinner for our parents.*

park
a piece of ground with trees and grass *Let's go to the park to play.*

park (parking, parked)
to put a car, truck, bus or bike in a place for a time *You can park right in front of the library.*

parrot
a tropical bird with coloured feathers *My parrot can say my name.*

part
1 one of the pieces or sections that something is divided into *Would you like part of my orange?*
2 the role of an actor in a film or a play *Who is playing the part of the princess?*

A B C D E F G H I J K L M

party (parties)

a group of people gathered together to enjoy themselves *The party is on Saturday.*

▼ party

pass (passing, passed)

1 to go beyond or past a person, place or thing *You'll pass the bakery on your way.*
2 to succeed in doing something such as a test or an examination *I hope you pass your driving test.*
3 to give someone something *Please pass the strawberries.*

passenger

someone who travels in a vehicle that is controlled by someone else *This plane has seats for 48 passengers.*

Passover

a Jewish holiday held in the spring. *All of the family get together for Passover.*

past

1 after *Let's meet at half past six.*
2 up to and beyond *The bank is on this street, just past the supermarket.*
3 the time before the present *In the past, there was no such thing as email.*

pasta

food made from flour, eggs and water, cut into shapes *Pasta is tasty.*

 pasta

N O P Q R S T U V W X Y Z

paste
1 a type of glue that is used for sticking paper *You can make paste with flour and water.*
2 a soft, spreadable mixture *He likes fish paste sandwiches.*

patch (patches)
1 material to cover a hole in something *I put a patch on my jeans.*
2 a small piece of land *We have a vegetable patch this summer.*

·Puzzle time·

What grows in a vegetable patch? Unscramble these words to find out!

1. tscrrao 2. bbcaaseg
3. ttoomaes 4. snaeb

answers: 1. carrots 2. cabbages 3. tomatoes 4. beans

pattern
1 lines, shapes or colours arranged in a certain way *The pattern that is on the cushions matches the pattern on the curtains.*
2 a shape that you copy or use as a guide to make something *Mum used a pattern to make this jacket for me.*

pavement
the path you walk on next to a road *The cycle path runs between the pavement and the road.*

paw
the foot of an animal *Our dog has a sore paw.*

pay (paying, paid)
to give someone money for something that you are buying, or because someone has done work for you *Don't worry, I'll pay for the theatre tickets.*

A B C D E F G H I J K L M

pea

a small, round green seed that is eaten as food *Would you like peas with your dinner?*

▶ peas

peace

1 no war or fighting *There has been peace between them for many years.*
2 quiet, calmness *She shut the door for a little peace and quiet.*

peach (peaches)

a soft fruit with a large seed inside it *This is a sweet, juicy peach.*

peacock

a male bird with long, brightly coloured tail feathers that spread out like a fan *Peacocks usually have green and blue feathers.*

peanut

a small nut with a soft, bumpy shell *Those peanuts taste very salty.*

pedal

1 part of a bicycle that you push with your feet to make the wheels go round *Can you reach the pedals?*
2 part of a car that you push with your feet to make it stop and go *The brake pedal is for stopping the car.*

peel (peeling, peeled)

to take the skin off a fruit or a vegetable *I helped peel the potatoes.*

pen

an object for drawing and writing with ink *Sign this with a black pen.*

▶ pencils

pencil

an object used for drawing and writing that has lead, not ink, in it *Do the crossword with a pencil.*

N O P Q R S T U V W X Y Z

penguin

a black and white sea bird that cannot fly *Penguins use their wings to help them swim.*

• Did you know? •

Penguins usually have one or two eggs at a time. Both parents take turns keeping the eggs warm. Later, the young are looked after in a group, usually by the males.

▲ penguins

penny (pence)

one pence *These sweets are a penny each.*

pepper

1 a hot powder used to flavour food *Please pass the salt and pepper.*
2 a sweet or hot-tasting vegetable *Peppers may be green, red, yellow or orange.*

perfume

a liquid with a pleasant smell that you put on your skin *What perfume are you wearing?*

person (people, persons)

a human being, a man, woman or child *Our geography teacher is a very interesting person.*

pet

an animal that is kept at someone's home *Do you have any pets?*

petrol

liquid fuel that makes a car engine run *We need to stop for petrol.*

A B C D E F G H I J K L M

phone (phoning, phoned)
to call someone on the telephone *Joe phoned while you were out.*

photo (photograph)
a picture made with a camera *We had our photos taken for our passports.*

piano
a musical instrument *I play the piano.*

▲ How many things can you see beginning with 'p'?

pick (picking, picked)
1 to choose *I was picked for the team.*
2 to break off a flower or a piece of fruit from a plant *I picked an apple.*
3 to pull pieces off or out of something *Pick the meat from the bone.*

picnic
food that you take outdoors to eat *We had a picnic in the park.*

picture
a drawing, painting or photograph *The winner's picture will be in the paper.*

pie
food made with fruit, vegetables, fish or meat that is baked inside pastry *Would you like another piece of pie?*

▶ pies

piece
a part of something that has been separated or broken *Careful, there are some pieces of glass on the floor.*

pig
an animal with pink skin and a curly tail *A baby pig is called a piglet.*

pile

a lot of things put on top of each other *There's a pile of clothes on the floor.*

▶ pineapple

pillow

a cushion to put your head on in bed *I put my tooth underneath my pillow.*

pilot

the person who is in control of a plane *The pilot showed us the plane's control panel.*

pin

a sharp, thin piece of metal that is used to fasten things or hold pieces of cloth together *Take all the pins out before you try that on.*

pineapple

a brown fruit that is yellow inside and has pointed leaves that stick out of the top *Pineapple juice is my favourite drink.*

pirate

a person who goes onto boats and ships to steal the things they are carrying *The ship was attacked by a group of pirates.*

pizza

a thin, flat round bread that is covered with tomatoes, cheese and other toppings then baked in an oven *We're going to have pizza at the party.*

place

where something is, the position, point or other location *What's the name of the place where we went on holiday last year?*

plain

1 one colour, having no pattern or decoration *The curtains are plain green.*
2 easy to understand *Can you tell me in plain English?*
3 not fancy or complicated *It's a plain room, but very clean and neat.*

plan

1 an idea about what will happen in the future *We have holiday plans.*
2 a drawing of a room, building or other space *We drew a plan of our playground.*

plane

an aeroplane *The plane took off from the airport on time.*

planet

one of the very large, round objects that moves around the Sun *There are nine planets in our Solar System.*

▼ planets

plan (planning, planned)

to think about what you want to do and how to do it *Let's plan a party.*

plant

a living thing that has roots, leaves and seeds and can make its own food *Water the plants every day.*

plant (planting, planted)
to put seeds or plants into the ground or containers so they will grow *Plant the seeds in early summer.*

plaster
1 a thick paste that hardens when it dries *Plaster is used to cover walls.*
2 a thin piece of plastic or cloth that you put over a cut or sore *I have a plaster on my knee.*

plastic
a light material that is made from chemicals *The bucket is made of plastic.*

plate
a flat dish to eat food from *Take the plates into the kitchen.*

play
a story performed by actors in a theatre or on the radio *The Tempest is a play full of magical things.*

play (playing, played)
to do things that you like such as games or sports *Let's play outdoors.*

▼ play

playground
a place for children to play *There are swings and a slide at the playground.*

please
a word to use when you are asking for something politely *Please wait here.*

plenty
enough or more than enough *Have one of my sandwiches, I have plenty.*

plough

a piece of equipment that farmers use to turn the soil before they plant *Modern ploughs can cut through the earth very quickly.*

plug

1 a piece of plastic or rubber that stops water going out of a sink or bath *Put the plug in the bath, then turn on the water.*
2 a piece of plastic connected to an electrical wire that you put into a wall *Which one is the plug for the computer?*

plumber

a person whose job it is to fix water taps and pipes *The plumber repaired the leak.*

plus (pluses)

and, added to, the symbol + *Eleven plus six equals seventeen,* $11 + 6 = 17$.

pocket

a small, flat bag sewn into a piece of clothing or luggage *Put your key in your pocket.*

poem

writing that uses words that sound good together. The words may rhyme *This poem is very funny.*

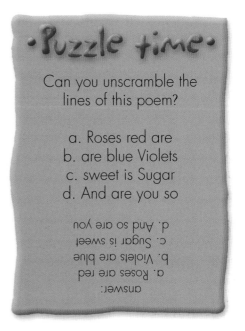

·Puzzle time·

Can you unscramble the lines of this poem?

a. Roses red are
b. are blue Violets
c. sweet is Sugar
d. And are you so

answer:
a. Roses are red
b. Violets are blue
c. Sugar is sweet
d. And so are you

N O P Q R S T U V W X Y Z

point
1 a sharp end on something *Use a pencil with a sharp point.*
2 a certain place or time *There's a meeting point at the airport.*
3 the reason for something *The whole point was to raise money for the school.*
4 a mark for counting a score in a game *The answer is worth one point.*

point (pointing, pointed)
to use your hand or finger to show someone something *Point to where the gate is.*

pole
a long narrow piece of wood, plastic or metal *We forgot to take the tent poles.*

police
people whose job it is to make sure everyone obeys the law *Police officers work very hard.*

polite
speaking or acting in a pleasant and not rude way *It is polite to say please, thank you and excuse me.*

pond
a small area of water *There are fish in the pond.*

pony (ponies)
a small horse *Dusty is a beautiful little pony.*

▶ pony

pool
1 a place filled with water for swimming *I like playing in my pool when the weather is warm.*
2 a puddle or another small area of water *We saw tiny, coloured fish in the pools on the beach.*

A B C D E F G H I J K L M

poor

1 not having enough money *It's a very poor country.*
2 not as good as it should be *The food was poor.*

pop

1 a sudden noise *There was a loud pop when they opened the bottle.*
2 a short form of popular *They are a famous pop band.*
3 a fizzy drink *Do you want a bottle of pop?*

porcupine

a wild animal with long bristles on its back *Porcupine bristles are very sharp.*

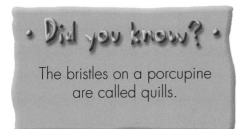

· Did you know? ·

The bristles on a porcupine are called quills.

porridge

a warm breakfast food that is made from oats *I like honey on porridge.*

post office

a place where people buy stamps and send letters *Can you get me some stamps at the post office?*

potato (potatoes)

a roundish white vegetable that grows under the ground *Potatoes have brown, yellow or red skins.*

pour (pouring, poured)

to make a liquid move out of or into something *Pour the juice while I make breakfast.*

powerful

1 having strength *A crocodile has powerful jaws.*
2 able to control *It is one of the most powerful countries in the world.*

practice
Something that you do again and again to improve a skill *What time is swimming practice tonight?*

practise (practising, practised)
doing something regularly to improve a skill *Keep practising your serve.*

pram
a little bed on wheels for moving a baby around *We're taking the baby out in the pram.*

prepare (preparing, prepared)
to get ready or to make something ready *I'm preparing for the test.*

present
▶ present
1 a gift, a thing that you are given without asking for it *Thank you for all the presents.*
2 now *The story is set in the present.*

president
the leader of an organisation or a country *She is president of the club.*

press (pressing, pressed)
to push something *Press the space bar.*

pretend (pretending, pretended)
to act like something is true when it is not *She pretended to be asleep.*

pretty
pleasant to look at *What pretty flowers!*

price
the amount of money that something costs *The prices are high.*

prince
the son or grandson of a king or queen *Prince Charming found the glass slipper.*

A B C D E F G H I J K L M

princess (princesses)
a daughter or the granddaughter of a king or queen *The princess dreamed of a faraway place.*

◀ princess

print (printing, printed)
1 to put letters, numbers or pictures on paper with a machine *Print five copies of the story.*
2 to write words without joining the letters *Print your name in full.*

printer
1 a machine connected to a computer that makes copies on paper *The printer is out of paper.*
2 a person who runs a printing machine *Take the poster to the printer.*

prison
a place where people are kept under guard as punishment *The thief was sent to prison.*

prize
something that you win in a game or competition *First prize is a holiday.*

problem
1 something that is wrong and needs to be corrected *We have a problem.*
2 a question that needs to be answered *There are problems at work.*

promise (promising, promised)
to tell someone that you will definitely do something *The boy promised he would be good.*

protect (protecting, protected)
to take care of someone or something and not let it be hurt or damaged *Penguins protect their chicks.*

N O **P** Q R S T U V W X Y Z

proud
feeling happy that you or someone else has done something, or has something *My parents are proud of me.*

puddle
a little pool of water on the ground or floor *There are puddles after the rain.*

pull (pulling, pulled)
to move something towards you or drag something behind you *We pulled on the rope as hard as we could.*

◀ pull

pump
a machine that moves a liquid or gas in a certain direction *Take your tyre pump with you.*

puncture
a hole made by a sharp object, especially in a tyre *We had a puncture on the way home.*

punish (punishing, punished)
to do something bad or unpleasant to someone because they have done something wrong *Don't punish him, it was an accident.*

pupil
1 a school student *The pupils at school wear uniforms.*
2 the black circle in the middle of your eye *Your pupil gets smaller when you look at bright light.*

puppet
a toy that people move by putting their hand inside it or by pulling strings attached to it *There's a puppet show starting on the beach in ten minutes.*

A B C D E F G H I J K L M

puppy (puppies)
a young dog
Puppies love to play.

▶ puppies

pure
not mixed with
anything else *This is pure apple juice.*

purr
the soft, low sound a cat makes
when it is happy *Our cat purrs when
you scratch his ears.*

purse
a bag to keep money in *I'll have to
pay you later, I left my purse at home.*

push (pushing, pushed)
1 to move something away from
you or out of the way *He pushed past
everyone.*
2 to press down on something such
as a key or a button *Push the restart
button.*

put (putting, put)
to move a thing to a place *Just put
the bags over there.*

pyjamas
loose clothes that you wear to bed
Have a bath and put on your pyjamas.

pyramid
1 a very old stone building with
triangular walls that form a point
at the top *The Egyptian pyramids
were built 4000 years ago.*
2 something with this shape *The
tent is pyramid-shaped.*

▶ python

python
a large snake that kills animals for
food by squeezing them *Some
pythons grow to be 8 metres long.*

quarter
one of four equal, or nearly equal, parts of something *Divide the apple into quarters.*

queen
the royal female ruler of a country or the wife of a king *The queen lives in a palace.*

▲ How many things can you see beginning with 'q'?

question
something that you ask someone *We'll try to answer all your questions.*

queue
a line of people waiting *There was a long queue at the cinema.*

quick (quickly)
fast *Email is quick and easy.*

quiet (quietly)
1 not making a noise *Please be quiet.*
2 calm and still, not busy *The lake is quiet and peaceful this time of day.*

· **Did you know?** ·

Elizabeth I (the first) was queen of England from 1558 to 1603. She was the youngest daughter of Henry VIII (eighth).

◀ queen

A B C D E F G H I J K L M

quilt

a warm cover for a bed *Patchwork quilts are made by sewing lots of small pieces of cloth together.*

quiz

a game or competition that tests your knowledge *We have a quiz night every year at Scouts.*

•Puzzle time•

Can you answer all the questions in this quiz?
1. What is a baby pig called?
2. Can penguins fly?
3. Is a tomato a fruit or a vegetable?
4. What are the spines on a porcupine called?

answers:
1. piglet 2. no 3. fruit 4. quills

▲ quilt

quit (quitting, quit)

to stop doing something or to leave a computer program *To quit, press Ctrl + Q.*

quote (quoting, quoted)

to repeat the words that someone else has said or written *The English teacher quoted a line from Shakespeare's* Hamlet *to the class.*

N O P Q R S T U V W X Y Z

Rr

rabbit

a small furry animal with long ears *There are rabbits living in the wood.*

▶ rabbits

race

1 a competition to see who can do something the fastest *The race starts in 15 minutes.*
2 a group of people with similar physical features *The goal is that people of all races and all beliefs can live together happily.*

race (racing, raced)

1 to compete in a race *They're racing against some of the fastest runners in the world.*
2 to do something very quickly *Jessie raced through the first part of the test.*

racket (racquet)

1 a flat, hard net on the end of a stick that you use to play sports such as tennis, badminton and squash *These new tennis rackets are very light.*
2 noise *Who's making all that racket?*

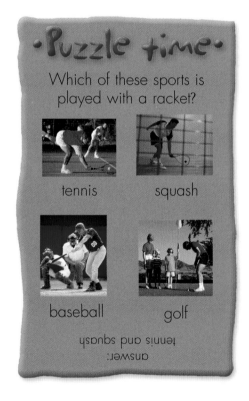

•Puzzle time•

Which of these sports is played with a racket?

tennis

squash

baseball

golf

answer:
tennis and squash

A B C D E F G H I J K L M

radio

a piece of equipment that receives sounds *I listen to the radio every day.*

▶ radio

rail

1 a bar to hang things on or stop things from falling *Put your wet towel on the rail to dry.*
2 one of two metal tracks that a train runs on *They put new rails all along the track.*

railway

1 a train track *The railway runs to the coast.*
2 a system of trains *A light railway is being built in the city.*

rain

water that falls from clouds in the sky *It's been raining all day.*

rainbow

the curve of colours that you see in the sky after it rains and the sun comes out *The colours of the rainbow are red, orange, yellow, green, blue, indigo and violet.*

raise (raising, raised)

to lift or put something in a higher place *Raise your hand if you know the answer.*

rat

an animal that looks like a big mouse with a long tail *There are rats in the barn*

▶ rat

rattle

a toy that makes a knocking noise when you shake it *Babies like rattles.*

N O P Q R S T U V W X Y Z

raw
not cooked *You can eat cabbage raw.*

◀ read

read (reading, read)
to understand words or symbols printed on a page *I like reading in the garden.*

record (recording, recorded)
to write down, tape or otherwise store information *We recorded our voices on the computer.*

recycle (recycling, recycled)
to use something over again *We're recycling newspapers and magazines at school.*

reflection
an image, like a copy of something, that is seen in a mirror or water *We could see the reflection of the mountain in the water.*

refrigerator (fridge)
a machine to keep food cool *Put the milk back in the refrigerator.*

▶ refrigerator

remember (remembering, remembered)
1 to keep information about the past in your mind *I remember how much fun we had then.*
2 to bring back information to your mind *I just remembered, I'm away then.*

remind (reminding, reminded)
to cause someone to remember something *Remind me to buy sugar.*

A B C D E F G H I J K L M

repeat (repeating, repeated)
to say or do something again *Sorry, could you repeat that – I didn't hear you.*

rescue (rescuing, rescued)
to save someone or something from danger *The lifeguard rescued the children.*

▶ rhinoceros

rest (resting, rested)
to not be active, to relax *I wasn't asleep, just resting.*

restaurant
a place where people eat and pay for meals *There's a new Thai restaurant in town.*

result
1 something that happens because of something else *This beautiful garden is the result of a lot of hard work.*
2 a final score *Have you heard the latest football results?*

return (returning, returned)
1 to come back or go back to a place *He returned after the meeting.*
2 to give or send something back *We returned the books to the library.*

rhinoceros (rhinoceroses)
a very large, wild animal with thick skin and a large horn on its nose *Rhinoceroses have very weak eyesight.*

rhyme (rhyming, rhymed)
when a word ends with the same sound as another word *Tree rhymes with three.*

▼ ribbon

ribbon
a narrow piece of cloth or paper for tying up presents or decorating things *What colour ribbon is on your dress?*

rice

grains from a plant that are boiled and eaten as food *We had pilau rice with our vegetable curry.*

rich

1 having a lot of money *We are not rich but we're very happy.*
2 food that has butter, cream and eggs is rich food *The cheese sauce is too rich for me!*
3 a deep or strong colour, smell or sound *The queen was wearing rich, purple robes.*

riddle

a difficult but funny question *Tom knows lots of riddles.*

ride (riding, rode, ridden)

to travel on and control the movement of a bicycle or a horse *Dad is teaching my little sister how to ride a bike.*

right

correct *You got all the answers right!*

▲ How many things can you see beginning with 'r'?

ring

1 a piece of jewellery worn on the finger *That's a pretty silver ring.*
2 a circle or something that is the shape of a circle *We put our chairs in a ring around the teacher.*
3 the sound made by a bell *The phone has a very loud ring.*
4 a telephone call *Give me a ring when you get home from work.*

river

a long line of water that flows to the sea *The Nile is the longest river.*

A B C D E F G H I J K L M

road

a track for vehicles such as cars and trucks to travel on *Some country roads are very narrow.*

roar

the sound a lion makes *There was a loud roar just outside the tent.*

robot

a machine that can do things that a person can do *My robot can play football.*

▶ robot

rock

1 the hard, stony part of the Earth's surface *They drilled through rock to find the oil.*
2 a large stone *We sat on the rocks and fished.*
3 a type of music that has a strong beat *My brother likes hard rock.*

rocket

1 a space vehicle shaped like a tube *The rocket is carrying valuable equipment to the space station.*
2 a tube-shaped firework *Rockets were exploding all over the sky.*

roll (rolling, rolled)

to move by turning over *The ball rolled across the pitch.*

roof

the outer covering over the top of a building or car *Rain leaked through the roof and onto the floor.*

room

part of a building that has its own floor, walls and ceiling *What's your room like?*

▶ rope

rope

very thick string *Tie the rope tightly.*

rose

a flower that grows on a stem with thorns *My mother loves roses.*

▲ roses

rough

1 uneven, not smooth *That bench is quite rough.*
2 not gentle *Don't be rough with the puppy.*

roundabout

1 a round place where roads meet *Turn left at the next roundabout.*
2 a round playground toy that children spin and ride on *Let's ride on the roundabout.*

route

the way to go to a place *We looked at the map and decided which route to take.*

row (rowing, rowed)

to move a small boat through water using long wooden poles that are wide at one end *We rowed the boat across the lake.*

royal

of or belonging to a queen or king *The people cheered as the royal procession marched through the town.*

rubber

1 a bouncy material that is made from the juice of a tree *Car tyres are made of rubber.*
2 a small object that is used for taking pencil marks off paper *I've made lots of mistakes on my homework, can I borrow your rubber?*

A B C D E F G H I J K L M

rubbish

1 paper and other things that are no longer needed *Rubbish goes in the bin.*
2 something that is bad, wrong or silly *The film was rubbish.*

· Did you know? ·

Recycling rubbish such as paper and glass is good for the environment.

rude

speaking or acting in a way that makes people feel bad *Don't be rude.*

rug

1 a small carpet *The cat is on the rug.*
2 a blanket *Put the rug over your feet.*

rule

a law or guide about how something must be done *It's wrong to break the rules at school.*

ruler

1 a long, flat piece of plastic or wood that has a straight edge and measurements *I use a ruler in maths.*
2 a person who has power over a country *The country has no ruler.*

▶ run

run (running, ran)

1 to move your legs faster than when you are walking *Run as fast as you can!*
2 to control *The business is run from home.*
3 to make a piece of equipment or a computer program work *Run the computer program.*

N O P Q **R** S T U V W X Y Z

Ss

sad
unhappy *What's happened? You look so sad.*

safe
not dangerous *Home is where you feel good and safe.*

sail
a large piece of strong material attached to a boat or ship, which catches the wind and makes the boat move across the water *The ship has many sails.*

▶ sails

sail (sailing, sailed)
to travel across water in a boat or ship *I am learning to sail a boat.*

salad
vegetables or fruit mixed together, usually eaten raw *We'll have a mixed salad.*

▶ salad

salt
very tiny grains that come from sea water and rocks, that are put on food to make it taste good *This needs a little more salt.*

same
not different or changed *Look, our clothes are exactly the same.*

sand
tiny pieces of crushed rock *The beach is covered in beautiful, white sand.*

sandwich (sandwiches)
two pieces of bread with cheese, meat or vegetables in between *We'll make some sandwiches for the picnic.*

A B C D E F G H I J K L M

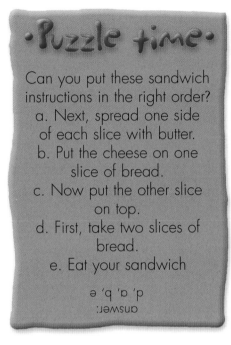

saucer
the small dish that goes under a cup
*We put some milk in a saucer for the
kittens.*

sausage
a mixture of meat, cereal and spices
that is shaped like a tube *Would you
like sausages with your breakfast?*

scales
a machine that is used for weighing
things *Weigh the ingredients on the
scales.*

scar
the mark left on your skin after a
cut has healed *I have a scar above
my left eye.*

scare (scaring, scared)
to frighten *This film will really scare
you!*

scarecrow
an object that is made to look like
a person, which is put in fields to
scare off birds so they don't eat the
crops *We've made our scarecrow out of
straw.*

scared
feeling afraid, frightened *Please leave
a light on, I'm scared of the dark.*

N O P Q R **S** T U V W X Y Z

school

the place where children go to study and be taught *I'm studying French at school.*

science

the study of information about the world *Biology, physics and chemistry are all kinds of science.*

score (scoring, scored)

to get points in a game *Goal! Goal! We've scored another goal!*

scorpion

an animal that has eight legs and a tail *Scorpions have a painful sting.*

• Did you know? •

Scorpions have been around for 4 million years.

◀ scorpion

scratch (scratching, scratched)

1 to rub your skin with your fingers or nails *Don't scratch your face.*
2 to damage an object by rubbing it with something *The car is scratched.*

▲ How many things can you see beginning with 's'?

scream (screaming, screamed)

to make a loud noise when you are afraid, angry or hurt *She screamed loudly.*

screen

1 the flat part of a computer or television that you look at *You're too close to the screen.*
2 a flat piece of material for showing films *The cinema has a screen.*

sea

a large area of salty water, sometimes called the ocean *Look, you can see the sea from here.*

seal

1 an animal that lives in the sea and eats fish *Seals are good swimmers and can dive underwater for a long time.*
2 wax, plastic or paper that you break to open a container or a document *Do not buy this product if the seal is broken.*

▼ seals

secret

something that you do not want other people to know *Please don't tell anyone else – it's a secret.*

see (seeing, saw, seen)

1 to use your eyes to look *We saw a deer.*
2 to understand *See? This is how it works.*
3 to watch *Did you see that programme on TV last night?*
4 to meet or visit someone *We went to see Chloe in hospital.*

seed

the part of a plant that a new plant grows from *Put the seeds in the ground.*

seesaw

a long board that is balanced in the middle so that the ends go up and down *There's a seesaw in the playground.*

send (sending, sent)

to make something go or be taken to another place *I sent her an email yesterday.*

sew (sewing, sewed, sewn)
to join cloth together with a needle and thread *I'll sew the button on for you.*

shade
1 where the sun is not shining *Sit in the shade of the umbrella.*
2 a thing to stop light *Can you pull the shade down, please?*
3 a colour *That's a nice shade of green.*

shake (shaking, shook, shaken)
to move something up and down or side to side quickly *Shake well before opening.*

shampoo
liquid soap for washing your hair *Did you bring the shampoo?*

shape
the outline or form of a thing *What shape is it?*

shark
a large fish that usually has sharp teeth *Some sharks can be dangerous to humans.*

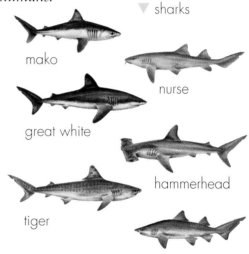

▼ sharks

mako

nurse

great white

hammerhead

tiger

sand

sheep (sheep)
a farm animal kept for wool and meat *There are sheep on the hill.*

shelf (shelves)
a board, usually wooden, fixed on a wall for putting things on *Can you reach that shelf?*

A B C D E F G H I J K L M

shell
the hard covering of an egg, a seed or an animal such as a turtle or a crab *Ostrich eggs are very big and have thick shells.*

ship
a large boat *The pirates filled the ship with treasure.*

▶ ship

shirt
a piece of clothing worn on the top half of your body *Tuck your shirt in.*

shock
1 a bad surprise *The bill was quite a shock.*
2 a pain you feel when electricity goes through your body *I got a shock from that plug!*

shoe
one of the things made of strong material that you wear on your feet *Wear comfortable shoes.*

shoot (shooting, shot)
1 to fire a weapon at someone or something *Don't shoot!*
2 to kick or throw a ball into a goal or net in a game *Shoot when you are closer to the basket.*

N O P Q R S T U V W X Y Z

shop

a place that sells things *What time does the shop open?*

short

1 not tall *He is short for his age.*
2 not long *She cut her hair short.*
3 not lasting a long time *Let's take a short break.*

shorts

short trousers *We wear our shorts in summer.*

▶ shorts

shoulder

the top of your arm where it joins your body *Put the bag over your shoulder.*

shout (shouting, shouted)

to call out to someone in a loud voice *There's no need to shout at me, I'm right here!*

show (showing, showed)

1 to let someone see something *Show me your new game.*
2 to guide someone somewhere or help them to do something *The guide showed us around.*

shower

1 something that you stand under to wash your body *Every room in the hotel has been fitted with a private shower.*
2 a light fall of rain *There will be showers in the afternoon.*

shrink (shrinking, shrank, shrunk)

to become smaller *My favourite skirt shrank in the wash.*

shut (shutting, shut)
to close *Shut the door, please.*

sideways
towards one side, not forwards or backwards *Turn sideways and then you can get past.*

sign (signing, signed)
to write your name on something *Sign at the bottom.*

silly
stupid, not reasonable *Don't be so silly!*

sing (singing, sang, sung)
to make music with your voice *Sing us a song.*

sink (sinking, sank, sunk)
to go down below the surface of water *The ship* Titanic *sank after it hit an iceberg.*

sister
a girl or woman who has the same parents as you *Julie is my younger sister.*

sit (sitting, sat)
to put your bottom on a chair or another type of seat *I must sit down, my feet ache.*

▼ skate

skate (skating, skated)
to move over ground or ice wearing boots with wheels or blades *He can skate well.*

skeleton

the bones in your body *He wore a suit with a skeleton painted on it for Hallowe'en.*

sketch (sketching, sketched)

to draw quickly *Artists sketch a scene first.*

▶ ski

ski (skiing, skied)

to move quickly over snow or water on long, narrow pieces of wood *Do you know how to ski?*

skirt

a piece of clothing worn by girls and women that hangs from the waist down *You can wear that skirt to school.*

sky (skies)

the space above you where the Sun, Moon, stars and clouds are *The sky was full of stars.*

slap (slapping, slapped)

to hit something with an open hand *She slapped his hand.*

sled (sledges)

a vehicle or toy for moving across ice or snow *We built a sled out of an old wooden box.*

sleep (sleeping, slept)

to not be awake *The baby is sleeping.*

▶ sleep

A B C D E F G H I J K L M

slide (sliding, slid)
to move across or down a smooth surface *The car slid across the ice.*

slippers
shoes that you wear indoors *Put your slippers on if your feet are cold.*

slow (slow)
not fast, taking a long time *This is a slow train.*

small
little or young *The jeans have a small pocket for coins.*

smile (smiling, smiled)
to make your mouth curve up and look happy *Why are you smiling?*

smoke
the cloudy gas that is made when something burns *The room filled with smoke.*

smooth
not rough or bumpy *You can skate on the pavement, it's smooth.*

snail
an animal that looks like a worm with a shell on its back *We have a lot of snails in our garden.*

Did you know?
The biggest snail ever found was an African giant snail – it was the size of a football!

snake
an animal that has a long body with no legs *Simon has a pet snake.*

sneeze (sneezing, sneezed)
to blow air out of your nose suddenly, with a loud noise *He's sneezing and coughing because he has a cold.*

snow

soft pieces of frozen water that fall from the sky *The trees are covered in snow.*

▼ snow

soap

something that you use with water to wash your body *Get a new bar of soap.*

soccer

football, a game played by two teams that try to get a round ball between two posts *A soccer team has 11 players.*

socks

pieces of clothing that you wear on your feet *Socks keep your feet warm.*

sofa

a long, soft seat for two or more people *Shall we sit on the sofa?*

▲ socks

soft

1 not hard *This bed is soft.*
2 not loud *She has a soft voice.*
3 smooth to touch *The rabbit has lovely, soft fur.*

software

the programs that run on a computer *He designs software.*

solid

hard, not a liquid or a gas, without spaces inside *The front door is made of solid wood.*

A B C D E F G H I J K L M

some
1 an amount of something that is not exact *Would you like some rice with your dinner?*
2 part of, but not all *Some of these apples are rotten.*

son
a male child *My daughter is at the same school as your son.*

song
a piece of music *The children sang songs in the school hall.*

sore
hurting or painful *Is the cut on your leg still sore?*

sorry
feeling bad and wanting to apologise for something you have done *Did she say sorry for making you late for work?*

soup
a liquid food made from meat or vegetables *Have a bowl of tomato soup.*

▶ soup

sour
having a taste like lemons, not sweet *This juice is sour.*

space
1 an empty or open place *Is there any space left?*
2 everything beyond the Earth's air *Space travel is very exciting.*

spade
a tool for digging *Turn the soil with a spade.*

spaghetti
long, thin strips of pasta *Ella likes spaghetti.*

speed
how fast something moves *At what speed are we travelling?*

spell (spelling, spelled)
to write or say the letters of a word in the correct order *How do you spell 'skateboard'?*

▶ spider

spider
a small animal with eight legs *There's a spider in the bath.*

spill (spilling, spilled, spilt)
to cause a liquid to fall to the ground accidentally *I spilled the drink on the carpet.*

.

spoon
an object with a handle and small bowl that is used for eating *Put the spoon to the right of the plate.*

sport
physical activities such as swimming and tennis *Swimming is a sport the whole family likes.*

▼ sport

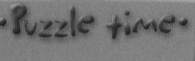

•Puzzle time•

Can you unscramble the names of these sports?

a. gruyb b. gsmwmin
c. cykeoh d. nintes

answers:
a. rugby b. swimming
c. hockey d. tennis

A B C D E F G H I J K L M

spring
the time of year between winter and summer *The cherry tree flowers in spring.*

squirrel
a small wild animal with a long, bushy tail *Squirrels are very good at climbing trees.*

stairs
steps in a building that go from one floor to another *I'll take the stairs to the office.*

▶ stars

stamp
1 a piece of paper that you buy to put on a letter or postcard before you post it *I'd like a first class stamp.*
2 a thing you put ink on and then press onto something to make a mark *The letter has a stamp on it.*

stand (standing, stood)
to be on your feet *She's standing by the door.*

star
1 a ball of burning gas that looks like a light in the sky *The stars are bright tonight*
2 a famous person *She's a big star now.*
3 a shape with five or six points *We baked biscuits shaped like stars.*

starfish (starfishes)
a star-shaped animal that lives in the sea *Starfish move very slowly.*

N O P Q R S T U V W X Y Z

start (starting, started)
to begin *I think it's time we made a start on the decorating.*

stay (staying, stayed)
1 to not leave a place *You stay here, I'll be right back.*
2 to live in a place for a short amount of time *When I was little, we stayed at my aunt's house every summer.*
3 to continue to remain the same *He's never grumpy, his mood stays the same all the time.*

steal (stealing, stole, stolen)
to take something that doesn't belong to you *The thieves stole my dad's car.*

stick
a long, thin piece of wood *We managed to make a fire by rubbing two sticks together.*

▶ stomach

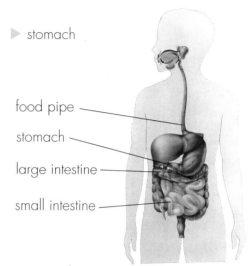

food pipe
stomach
large intestine
small intestine

stomach
the part inside your body where food goes when you eat *Another word for stomach is tummy.*

stone
1 rock *There is a stone floor in the castle.*
2 fourteen pounds or 6.35 kilograms *What is your weight in stones?*
3 the seed in some fruits *Careful, the cherries have stones in them.*

A B C D E F G H I J K L M

stool

a seat with no back *Sit on the stool.*

stop (stopping, stopped)

1 to quit doing something *Stop talking for a minute.*
2 to quit moving *Stop for the red light.*
3 to prevent something happening *The teacher stopped the fight.*

story (stories)

a description of events that may be real or imaginary *Everyone knows the story of Peter Pan.*

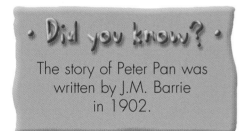

· Did you know? ·
The story of Peter Pan was written by J.M. Barrie in 1902.

straight not crooked or bent *She has very straight hair.*

strange

1 unusual *He's a strange-looking man.*
2 unfamiliar *He told a very strange story.*

strawberry strawberry (strawberries)

a soft, heart-shaped red fruit *You can pick the strawberries yourself on some farms.*

▶ strawberries

stream

a small river *We drank water from a mountain stream.*

stretch (stretching, stretched)

1 to get longer or bigger *Tights can stretch quite a bit.*
2 to straighten parts of your body *She stretched her legs out under the table.*

string

thick thread or thin rope *Tie some string around the box.*

◀ string

strong

1 powerful *Climbers have strong legs.*
2 not easily broken or damaged *The metal case is very strong.*

▶ Sun

stupid

not sensible or clever *What a stupid idea!*

submarine

a ship that can travel underwater *Submarines can help us to find out about underwater life.*

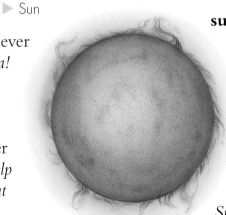

sudden

happening quickly and unexpectedly *There was a sudden explosion.*

sugar

a sweet substance used to flavour food *Sugar is made from plants.*

suitcase

a case or bag to carry clothes in when you travel *We have a suitcase with wheels.*

summer

the time of year between spring and autumn *Are you going on holiday this summer?*

Sun

the very bright star that the Earth travels around *All the planets in the Solar System travel around the Sun.*

A B C D E F G H I J K L M

supermarket
a large shop that sells food and other things *The supermarket stays open late on Fridays.*

surprise
something that is completely unexpected *An email from you! What a nice surprise!*

sweep (sweeping, swept)
to brush dirt from the floor or ground *Have you swept the kitchen?*

sweet
1 tasting sugary *These strawberries are very sweet.*
2 nice or pleasant *That's a sweet thing to say.*

swim (swimming, swam, swum)
to move through or across water by using your arms and legs *I can swim a whole length of the pool.*

▲ swing

swing (swinging, swung)
to move backwards, forwards or from side to side from a fixed point *I like swinging, it's lots of fun.*

sword
a very large knife that is used for fighting *'Excalibur' is the name of a famous sword.*

N O P Q R S T U V W X Y Z

T-shirt/t-shirt

a shirt with short sleeves, no collar and no buttons *Put a T-shirt on, it's warm today.*

table

1 a piece of furniture with legs and a flat top *Please clear the table.*

▲ table

2 a list of things such as numbers or words arranged in rows and columns *There's a table of prices and times.*

tail

the part of an animal at the end of its back *The dog has a long, white tail.*

◀ tail

take (taking, took, taken)

1 to carry something *Take an umbrella.*

2 to move something or someone to another place *Take this note to Mrs. Burnett.*

3 to steal *The thieves took all the money.*

talk (talking, talked)

to speak *Who were you talking to on the telephone last night?*

tall

1 higher than normal *My Grandad is tall, I am short.*

2 having a certain height *The fence is one metre tall.*

tank

1 a container for liquids *There's a leak in the petrol tank.*

2 a large fighting vehicle *Tanks are used in wars.*

A B C D E F G H I J K L M

tap
something that controls the flow of a liquid or gas *Turn the tap off.*

tape
1 a long, flat, narrow piece of plastic used for recording sounds or images, or the plastic container it is in *Can I borrow the tape?*
2 flat, narrow plastic that is sticky on one side *Put some tape on the package.*

taste (tasting, tasted)
1 to have a flavour *What does the soup taste like?*
2 to try a little food or drink to see what it is like *Have you tasted the pizza?*

taxi
a car that takes people to different places, for money *We'll take a taxi.*

tea
1 leaves that are used to make a drink or the drink made from these leaves *Pour the tea.*
2 the evening meal *What's for tea?*

teacher
a person who gives lessons in a subject *Kate's an art teacher.*

team
1 a group of people who play a game together *Which team are you on?*
2 a group of people who work together on a project *We have a great team.*

tear
a drop of water that comes out of your eye *Tears ran down his face.*

◀ taxi

N O P Q R S T U V W X Y Z

tear (tearing, tore, torn)
to rip, split or make a hole in
something *Tear the paper in half.*

teddy
a toy animal that looks like a bear
My teddy is soft and cuddly.

telephone
a piece of equipment that you use to
speak to someone in another place
Where's your telephone?

▶ telescope

telescope
a piece of equipment that
you use to look at things
that are far away *Look
through the telescope.*

television (TV)
a machine that shows
programmes *What's on television?*

·Puzzle time·

Can you match these star
patterns to the names below?
1. Pegasus (the winged
horse)
2. Ursa Major (Great Bear)
3. Hercules
4. Orion (the Hunter)

a

b

c

d

answers:
1d 2b 3a 4c

A B C D E F G H I J K L M

tell (telling, told)
1 to pass on information *I told you that story yesterday.*
2 to understand *I can't tell what it means.*

◀ tennis

tennis
a game played by two or four people who hit a ball over a net to score points *Tennis is a very fast game.*

tent
a temporary house, made of cloth or plastic, that is used for camping *The tent will keep us dry.*

terrible
very bad *That's terrible!*

test
1 a set of questions to measure knowledge *You must study carefully for the test.*
2 a set of checks to find out if something is safe or good to use *Cars must pass several tests.*

thank (thanking, thanked)
to tell someone you are pleased about something they have given you or have done for you *Remember to thank them.*

theatre
a building where you can go and see plays *Shall we go to the theatre this weekend?*

thick
1 not thin *The entrance was covered by a thick sheet of plastic.*
2 not watery *Make a thick paste from flour and water.*

N O P Q R S T U V W X Y Z

thief (thieves)
a person who steals *The bank was robbed by a gang of thieves.*

▲ How many things can you see beginning with 't'?

thin
1 having not much distance from one side to the other *Cut the paper into thin strips.*
2 not fat *She's quite thin.*
3 watery *It's a thin, clear soup.*

think (thinking, thought)
1 to use your mind to consider or remember something *Let me think.*
2 to have an opinion, to believe *I think we should try it.*

thirsty
feeling that you need to drink something *Are you thirsty?*

through
from one side to the other *Look through the window.*

throw (throwing, threw)
to make something go through the air *Throw the ball through the net.*

thumb
the finger on the inside of your hand *I've cut my thumb.*

thunder
the loud noise you can hear during a storm *As the storm broke we heard a very loud clap of thunder.*

ticket
a piece of paper that shows you have paid *I have tickets for the game.*

A B C D E F G H I J K L M

tidy
neat and organised *Mandy's room is never tidy.*

tie (tying, tied)
to join pieces of string, rope or thread together *Tie your shoelaces up.*

tiger
a large, wild cat that has black stripes on its yellow fur *The tiger's coat is black and orange.*

· Did you know? ·

Tigers are the biggest members of the cat family.

▶ tiger

tight
1 close-fitting *That looks a bit tight.*
2 firmly in place *Is it shut tight?*

tights
clothing worn on the legs *I wear tights to ballet.*

timetable
a list of things and the time they happen *Check the timetable.*

tired
feeling that you need to rest *The baby is tired.*

toast
bread that has been cooked in a toaster or a grill *I'll make some toast for breakfast.*

today
this day *What's the date today?*

N O P Q R S T U V W X Y Z

toe
one of the five parts of your body at the end of your foot *Ouch, I stubbed my toe.*

together
1 joined or mixed *Mix the eggs and milk together.*
2 with each other *Shall we go together?*

toilet
lavatory *Where's the toilet?*

tomato (tomatoes)
a red fruit that can be eaten raw or cooked *Put tomatoes in the salad.*

◀ tomatoes

tool
a piece of equipment that you use to do a job *Hammers and saws are tools.*

tooth (teeth)
one of the hard, white things in your mouth *You should brush your teeth twice a day.*

▼ tooth

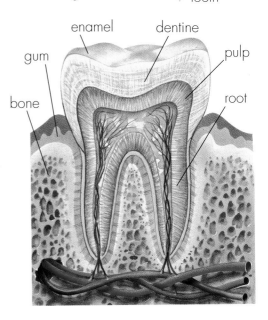

enamel
dentine
gum
pulp
bone
root

tongue
the soft part of your body that is inside your mouth that you use to speak with and to taste things *The ice cream feels cold on my tongue.*

A B C D E F G H I J K L M

top
1 the highest part of something
I've hidden the presents on top of the wardrobe.
2 a toy that balances on a point
Let's spin the top.
3 a cover for the upper body *That's a pretty top.*
4 a cover for a container *Put the top back on.*

torch
a light powered by batteries *Shine the torch over here.*

tortoise
a land animal that can pull its head and legs into the shell that covers its body *Tortoises can only move very slowly.*

touch (touching, touched)
1 to put your fingers or hand on something *Please don't touch the paintings.*
2 to be so close to another thing that there is no space between the two *The wires are touching.*

towel
a cloth that you use to dry things or your body with *Dry your hands on the towel.*

town
a place with houses and other buildings where people live and work *Our town has a good selection of shopping facilities.*

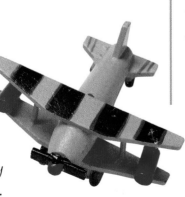

◀ toy

toy
something that children like to play with *Can I play with my toy plane?*

N O P Q R S T U V W X Y Z

tractor
a big vehicle that is used on a farm
Tractors are very powerful.

traffic lights
lights where two or more roads meet
that change colour, telling you
when to stop and go *Turn
left at the traffic lights.*

train
a line of
carriages pulled
by an engine on a
track *Trains travel at a fast speed.*

trainers
sports shoes *I bought some new trainers.*

**transport (transporting,
transported)**
to move people or things from one
place to another *The tanker transports
fuel.*

trap (trapping, trapped)
to catch something in a piece of
equipment *It traps mice.*

◀ train

**travel (travelling,
travelled)**
to go from one place to another
They're travelling by car.

treasure
a collection of valuable things
The chest is filled with treasure.

tree
a large, tall plant with a trunk and
branches *It's fun to climb trees.*

trick
1 something done to entertain
people *That was a clever trick.*
2 something done to fool or cheat
someone *That was a mean trick.*

A B C D E F G H I J K L M

trip (tripping, tripped)
to catch your foot on something, to stumble *Be careful – you could trip on the step.*

trip
a journey *We've decided to go on a trip around the world.*

trousers
clothing that covers the legs *He's wearing grey trousers.*

▶ truck

truck
a vehicle for carrying loads *We were stuck behind a truck.*

trunk
1 the main part of a tree *Palm trees have thick trunks.*
2 an elephant's nose *The elephant has a long trunk.*
3 a box for storing things in *Where's the key for this trunk?*

try (trying tried)
1 to make an effort *I tried to ring you.*
2 to test or sample something *Have you tried the pasta?*

tunnel
a long hole underground *There is a secret tunnel.*

turn
1 to move so you are looking or going in a new direction *Turn away.*
2 to move something to a different position *Turn the dial.*

turtle
an animal that lives in water that can pull its head and legs into the shell on its back *Turtles are reptiles.*

N O P Q R S T U V W X Y Z

Uu

ugly
not nice to look at *What an ugly colour!*

umbrella
a piece of equipment made of cloth stretched over a frame that keeps the rain off *It's raining outside – I'll take my umbrella.*

▲ umbrella

uncle
your mother's or father's brother, or your aunt's husband *He looks like his uncle.*

under
below, to a lower place *Put your bag under your seat.*

understand (understanding, understood)
1 to know the meaning of words or ideas *Does he understand English?*
2 to know how something works *Doctors understand the disease.*
3 to know how and why someone feels or acts a certain way *You don't understand.*

· Did you know? ·

You can understand words from other languages. From Italian we get the words balcony, giraffe and violin. From Spanish we get banana and guitar. From French we get chocolate, crocodile and medicine.

A B C D E F G H I J K L M

underwear
pieces of clothing that you wear next to your body, under your other clothes *Pack some underwear.*

▲ How many things can you see beginning with 'u'?

unhappy
not happy, sad *Cheer up, try not to look so unhappy.*

▶ unhappy

▲ uniforms

uniform
clothes worn by everyone in a group of people *Everyone wore uniforms.*

up
towards a higher position *Pass that brush up to me.*

upset
1 feeling worried, sad or angry *I didn't mean to upset you.*
2 feeling sick *His stomach is upset.*

upstairs
towards or on the upper floors of a building *Take these papers upstairs.*

N O P Q R S T U V W X Y Z

Vv

valley
the low land between two hills *There is a river in the valley.*

van
a small truck *The delivery van is here.*

vanish (vanishing, vanished)
to disappear *The deer suddenly vanished.*

vase
a container to hold water in *The vase is hand-painted.*

vegetable
a plant grown for food *Vegetables are healthy foods.*

vehicle
a machine which carries people or things *Trucks and trains are vehicles.*

vest
an undershirt *Put a vest on, it's cold today.*

vet (veterinary surgeon)
an animal doctor *The vet is treating our dog.*

▶ vet

▼ vase

video (video cassette recorder)
a machine for recording or playing TV programmes *Switch the video on.*

village
a group of houses and buildings in the country *It's a beautiful old village.*

A B C D E F G H I J K L M

vinegar

a liquid that is used to preserve food, or add flavour *Put vinegar on your chips.*

violin

a musical instrument that is played with a bow *My brother is learning to play the violin.*

▶ violin

virus (viruses)

1 a very tiny living thing that causes disease and illness *Flu is caused by a virus.*
2 a computer program that can damage files *The virus has damaged my files.*

visit (visiting, visited)

to go to see a person or a place *You can visit us this evening.*

voice

the sounds a person makes when speaking or singing *I didn't recognise your voice.*

volcano (volcanoes)

a mountain with an opening that sprays out steam or lava *The volcano is very active.*

vote (voting, voted)

to show which idea or person you choose by raising your hand or writing on paper *Let's take a vote on this idea.*

How many things can you see beginning with 'v'?

N O P Q R S T U V W X Y Z

Ww

waiter

a man or woman who serves food in a restaurant or café *Call the waiter, I want to pay.*

▶ waiter

waitress

a woman who serves food in a restaurant or café *Ask the waitress for the bill.*

wake (waking, woke, woken)

to stop being asleep *Wake up!*

walk (walking, walked)

to move along, putting one foot in front of the other *Let's walk together*

wall

1 the sides of a room or a building *There are several pictures on the wall.*
2 a structure made of stone or brick that divides a space *There's a brick wall around the garden.*

wand

a magic stick that fairies, witches and magicians use to do magic tricks *She waved her wand and turned the pumpkin into a coach.*

want (wanting, wanted)

to wish, desire or need something *Do you want a sandwich?*

wardrobe

a cupboard to hang clothes in *It's a big wardrobe.*

warm

slightly hot, not cool or cold *The water is lovely and warm.*

A B C D E F G H I J K L M

wash (washing, washed)
to clean with water *Wash your face.*

▶ wasp

wasp
a black and yellow flying insect that stings *Wasps live in nests.*

wastepaper bin
a container to put unwanted paper and rubbish in *Empty the wastepaper bin.*

watch
a small clock that you wear on your wrist *I'd like a watch for my birthday.*

watch (watching, watched)
to look at something and pay attention *We're watching TV.*

water
a liquid that falls from the sky as rain *Have a glass of water.*

waterfall
water from a stream or a river that falls straight down over rocks *There is a pool under the waterfall.*

wave
1 a raised part of moving water on the sea *Waves crashed on the beach.*
2 a movement of your hand to say goodbye, hello or get someone's attention *Give them a wave.*
3 the way light and sound move *Sound is carried on radio waves.*

▲ wave

weak
not strong *I feel weak and dizzy.*

wear (wearing, wore)
to have something, such as clothes, on your body *What shall I wear to the party?*

weather
the condition of the air – how hot or cold it is, the wind, rain and clouds *What's the weather like today?*

web
1 the very thin strings a spider weaves *A spider catches food in its web.*
2 the World Wide Web on the Internet *Do you use the Web?*

week
seven days *See you next week!*

weigh (weighing, weighed)
1 to measure how heavy something is *Weigh the fruit.*
2 to be heavy or light *How much do you weigh?*

well
1 in a good way *Well done!*
2 healthy, not ill *Get well soon.*

wet
not dry *Your hair's still wet.*

whale
a very large sea animal *Whales are mammals, not fish.*

▲ whale

wheel
a round object that turns and moves a vehicle along *The wheel came off the bike.*

whisper (whispering, whispered)
to speak very quietly so other people can't hear *Whisper the secret to me.*

A B C D E F G H I J K L M

whistle (whistling, whistled)
to blow air out through your lips
and make a sound *Can you whistle?*

wicked
very bad or evil *The wicked witch
trapped them.*

wife (wives)
the woman that a man is married to
His wife is very nice.

win (winning, won)
to be the first or the best in a race or
other competition *He's won the race!*

◀ win

wind
air moving across the ground *The
wind is strong.*

window
a glass-covered opening in a
building *Look out of the window.*

▲ winter

winter
the time of year between autumn
and spring *The weather can be very cold
in winter.*

wish (wishing, wished)
to hope for or want something *What
did you wish for?*

N O P Q R S T U V **W** X Y Z

witch (witches)

a woman who is supposed to have magic powers *The witches huddled over their big, black pot, making spells.*

• Did you know? •

Witches have been around for hundreds of years. Witchcraft was once an ancient religion. Modern witches do exist, but they don't fly around on broomsticks!

wizard

a man who is supposed to have magic powers *The wizard broke the spell.*

wolf (wolves)

a wild animal that looks like a large dog *They heard the wolf howling at the moon.*

woman (women)

a female adult *Are there women on the team?*

wonder (wondering, wondered)

to think about something and why it is that way *I wonder why she said that?*

wood

1 the material that a tree is made of *Put more wood on the fire.*
2 a small forest *We walked through the wood.*

wool

1 hair that grows on animals, such as sheep. *The wool is thick and warm.*
2 thread made from animal's hair *Get me a ball of wool.*

◀ wizard

A B C D E F G H I J K L M

work (working, worked)

1 to do a job *Does she enjoy her work as a doctor?*
2 to go or operate smoothly *This machine is working properly now.*

·Puzzle time·

Match the workers with the things they need to do their jobs

A | B
actor | paint
artist | theatre
pilot | menu
waiter | plane

answers: actor/theatre artist/paint pilot/plane waiter/menu

world

the Earth, the planet that we live on and everything that is on it *The Nile is the longest river in the world.*

worm

a long, thin animal with no legs that lives in earth *Worms are good for the soil.*

▶ worm

worry (worrying, worried)

to have the feeling that something bad might happen *You shouldn't worry, it's not a problem.*

worse (worst)

less than good *My cold is worse.*

write (writing, wrote)

1 to make a new story, poem, play, song or book *I wrote her a letter.*
2 to make letters, numbers and words *Write your name in the diary.*

wrong

not right, incorrect *We've made a wrong turn.*

How many things can you see beginning with 'x', 'y' and 'z'?

X-ray

1 a beam of energy that can go through solid things *X-rays are used at airports.*

2 a photograph of the inside of the body *The X-ray shows that his hand may be broken.*

▶ xylophone

xylophone

a musical instrument that is played by hitting flat, wooden or metal bars with a pair of sticks *The word xylophone comes from the Greek words 'xylo' (wood) and 'phone' (sound).*

yacht

a sailing boat *Yacht races are exciting.*

yawn (yawning, yawned)

to open your mouth and take a deep breath, usually when you are tired or bored *I can't stop yawning – I'm going to bed.*

year

a period of time that is equal to 12 months, especially from January to December *We're moving to a new house early next year.*

A B C D E F G H I J K L M

yes

a word that is used to say that you want something, that you will do something, that you agree with something or that something is true *Yes, I'd love to come to the cinema with you this evening.*

yesterday

the day before today *I phoned you yesterday.*

yoga

exercises for your body and mind *Yoga can help the body stay fit and healthy.*

yoghurt (yogurt)

a food made from milk *I'd like a strawberry yoghurt.*

young

not old *You're too young to walk to school on your own.*

yo-yo

a toy that moves up and down on a string that you hold in your hand *This yo-yo glows in the dark.*

▶ yo-yo

zebra

a wild, black-and-white striped horse *Zebras live in Africa.*

zero

nothing, 0 *The temperature is zero degrees.*

zip

a fastener made of two rows of teeth that lock together *My zip has broke.*

zoo

a place where wild animals are kept so that people can look at them and study them *We went to the zoo.*

N O P Q R S T U V W X Y Z

The publishers would like to thank the following artists who have contributed to this book:

Lisa Alderson, Julie Banyard, Martin Camm, Jim Channell, Kuo Kang Chen, Mark Davis, Nicholas Forder, Mike Foster, Luigi Gallante, Peter Gregory, Alan Hancocks, Ron Haywood, Sally Holmes, Richard Hook, Rob Jakeway, Tony Kenyon, Sue King, Steve Kirk, Mick Loates, Kevin Madison, Alan Male, Janos Marffy, Josephine Martin, Tracy Morgan, Gill Platt, Terry Riley, Andy Robinson, Mike Saunders, Peter Sarson, Rob Sheffield, Guy Smith, Roger Smith, Mike Taylor, Peter Taylor, Mike White, Colin Woolf

The publishers would like to thank the following for supplying photographs for this book:
Corbis: Reuters New Media 173 (t/l)

All other pictures: Corel, DigitalSTOCK, PhotoDisc